WHEN WORK WORKS

WHEN WORK WORKS

**CUTTING EDGE SOLUTIONS
FOR THE CONTEMPORARY WORKPLACE**

EDITED BY CATHY FYOCK AND EVERETT O'KEEFE

CINDY LUNDIN - DANA GRINDAL - CINDY SCHULER
MICHELE FANTT HARRIS - NICOLE HOLLAR - RALPH DE CHABERT
ERIC L. WILLIAMSON - CHRISTINA REISING - WENDY A. COCKE
DOUG REITZ - JEFF NALLY - AMY OVIEDO - MOLLEY RICKETTS
S. RICHARD PARK - PAMELA D. GREY

Copyright © 2024, Cathy Fyock

All rights reserved. No part of this book may be used or reproduced by any means, graphic, electronic, or mechanical (including any information storage retrieval system) without the express written permission from the author, except in the case of brief quotations for use in articles and reviews wherein appropriate attribution of the source is made.

Publishing support provided by
Ignite Press
55 Shaw Ave. Suite 204
Clovis, CA 93612
www.IgnitePress.us

ISBN: 979-8-9851961-3-9
ISBN: 979-8-9851961-4-6 (E-book)

For bulk purchases and for booking, contact:

Cathy Fyock
Cathy@CathyFyock.com

Because of the dynamic nature of the Internet, web addresses or links contained in this book may have been changed since publication and may no longer be valid. The content of this book and all expressed opinions are those of the author and do not reflect the publisher or the publishing team. The author is solely responsible for all content included herein.

Library of Congress Control Number: 2024910827

Cover design by Christopher Pana
Edited by Elizabeth Arterberry
Interior design by Jetlaunch

FIRST EDITION

The Authors

Cindy Lundin
Professional Leadership Coach, Speaker, and Workshop Facilitator

🌐 created2thrivecl.com

in linkedin.com/in/cindy-lundin-65383a208

f facebook.com/CindyLundincreated2thrivecl

Dana Grindal
Prayer Minister, Founder of Whitestone Ministries Intl

🌐 danagrindal.com

🌐 teachingfellowshipinstitute.org

🌐 fearlessandfreecommunity.com

in linkedin.com/in/dana-grindal-910084277

Cindy Schuler
Human Resources Consultant, Leadership Coach, Speaker, Facilitator

- linkedin.com/in/cindys1
- integristarhrconsulting.com
- integristarhrconsulting.com/when-work-works

Michele Fantt Harris, SHRM-SCP
Leadership and Career Coach

- michele.harris19@gmail.com
- linkedin.com/in/MicheleFanttHarris

Nicole Hollar
Empowerment and Wellness Speaker | Coach | Author

- nicolehollar.com
- linktr.ee/nicolehollar
- shorturl.at/mort4
- shorturl.at/dowHV

Ralph de Chabert

linkedin.com/in/ralph-de-chabert-18b2055

facebook.com/ralph.dechabert

Eric L. Williamson
Consultant, Speaker, Jerk Expert

tailoredtrainingsolutions.com

linkedin.com/in/eric-williamson-57976b9

twitter.com/TTS_Williamson

Christina Reising, SPHR, SHRM-CP
Positivity Instigator & Innovation Igniter

linkedin.com/in/christinareising

orbitcoachingandconsulting.com

Wendy A. Cocke
Founder - Engineering Leadership Solutions

🌐 engineeringleadershipsolutions.com

🌐 makingflexwork.com

🌐 reimagineyourwork.com

Doug Reitz
Dad, Husband, Builder, Speaker, Owner of MWC

in linkedin.com/in/doug-reitz

🌐 Dougreitz.blog

Jeff Nally, PCC, SHRM-SCP
Chief Coaching Officer, Chief Human Resources Officer, Executive Coach & Professional Speaker

🌐 nallygroup.com/whenworkworks

🌐 nallygroup.com

🌐 https://coachsource.com/

in linkedin.com/in/jeffnally

Amy Oviedo
Founder, Recruiting Experiences

🌐 recruitingexperiences.com

in linkedin.com/in/amyoviedo

in linkedin.com/company/recruitingex

f facebook.com/RecruitingExperiences

Molley Ricketts
CEO & Founder of Incipio Workforce Solutions

🌐 incipioworks.com

f facebook.com/IncipioWorks

in linkedin.com/in/molleyricketts

S. Richard Park, Ph.D.
Principal - Talent Alignment, LLC

🌐 talentalignment.net

in linkedin.com/in/rickpark

Dr. Pamela D. Grey

Thought Leader on How to Make Your Best Decisions and Premier Mentor to Women in Business

poweryourdecisions.com

facebook.com/power.your.decisions

instagram.com/power.your.decisions

Table of Contents

INTRODUCTION 1

CHAPTER 1: Faith-Filled Leadership: Integrating Faith within Coaching, Training, and Leadership 3
    BY CINDY LUNDIN

CHAPTER 2: Putting Your Heart into Your Work: How to Invest in the Hearts of Others without Missing Your Own 17
    BY DANA GRINDAL

CHAPTER 3: Will They Stay or Will They Go?: Recruiting and Retaining Talent through the Full Life Cycle of Employment . . . 29
    BY CINDY SCHULER

CHAPTER 4: Lead Them Before They Leave *You* 43
    BY MICHELE FANTT HARRIS, SHRM-SCP

CHAPTER 5: Playing Nice in the Sandbox: Workplaces Function Best When Everyone on the Team Is Mindful, Has Healthy Boundaries, and Demonstrates Respect 57
    BY NICOLE HOLLAR

CHAPTER 6: Employee Resource Groups: Barriers and Improving Impact 71
    BY RALPH DE CHABERT

CHAPTER 7: Creating a Jerk-Free Workplace through Courage . . . 85
    BY ERIC L. WILLIAMSON

Chapter 8: Mind Games: Unraveling the Mystery of Emotional Shenanigans with Mustard and Bananas 99
    by Christina Reising, SPHR, SHRM-CP

Chapter 9: Making Hybrid Work: Facilitating the Right Work from the Right Place at the Right Time 113
    by Wendy A. Cocke

Chapter 10: Be a Builder in Everything You Do Every Day 127
    by Doug Reitz

Chapter 11: Crafting Intentional Interactions at Work: In-Person Gatherings to Solve Business Problems and Cultivate Workplace Culture 141
    by Jeff Nally, PCC, SHRM-SCP

Chapter 12: All Guts? No Glory: Stop Relying on Referrals, Gut Feel, and Luck to Hire Top Talent 155
    by Amy Oviedo

Chapter 13: Empowering the Frontline: When Work Works for Those Who Matter Most 167
    by Molley Ricketts

Chapter 14: "So, What Do You Do?": The Answer Your CEO Will Love! 181
    by S. Richard Park, Ph.D.

Chapter 15: What Every Mentor Knows: "You Can't Google This Stuff!" 201
    by Dr. Pamela D. Grey

Conclusion 213

• • •

Introduction

Welcome to *When Work Works*, an anthology that delves into the question: What makes work truly work? In a world where the nature of work is continuously evolving, this volume harnesses the collective wisdom of fifteen diverse thought leaders from various industries and roles. Their insights navigate the multifaceted landscape of high-performing organizations, shedding light on the numerous factors that shape contemporary work environments.

An anthology like this is uniquely powerful because it brings together a tapestry of perspectives and insights. Each contributor offers a distinct viewpoint, underscoring the idea that there is no one-size-fits-all solution to creating effective and fulfilling work environments. This diversity of thought enriches our understanding and presents a more comprehensive picture of what it takes to foster success in today's workplaces.

As you turn the pages, you'll explore themes that are crucial to the modern workplace: culture and well-being, work/life balance, flexibility, diversity, inclusion, belonging, personal and professional development, and even the role of spirituality in work. Each chapter stands as a testament to the varied approaches organizations can take to achieve excellence, demonstrating that the path to a thriving workplace is as unique as the people who inhabit it.

Our contributors share their experiences and ideas on redefining workplace culture, prioritizing employee well-being, embracing flexible work arrangements, and championing diversity and inclusion. Their narratives are not just informative but also actionable, offering a wealth of ideas and strategies for creating optimal workplaces.

This anthology is more than just a collection of essays; it's an invitation to reconsider conventional notions of work and to embrace innovative strategies for building thriving organizations. Whether you are a leader, an HR professional, or someone passionate about the future of work, When Work Works offers a compelling read filled with practical insights and inspiration for fostering success in a rapidly changing landscape.

Join us on this journey to discover what truly makes work work, and how we can collectively shape a better, more effective, and more fulfilling world of work.

Everett O'Keefe and Cathy Fyock, SPHR

Chapter 1

Faith-Filled Leadership: Integrating Faith within Coaching, Training, and Leadership

Cindy Lundin

Professional Leadership Coach, Speaker, and Workshop Facilitator

created2thrivecl.com

linkedin.com/in/cindy-lundin-65383a208

facebook.com/CindyLundincreated2thrivecl

Cindy Lundin coaches, speaks, and advocates, cultivating hope, growth, and leadership. Grounded in her faith-filled journey and personal experiences, her coaching approach is characterized by commitment, passion, and a deep understanding of human dynamics. She empowers individuals, teams, and ministry groups to realize their full potential by leveraging their unique gifts and strengths.

From her tenure as a trusted loan officer in the financial industry to engaging in transformative ministry work, Cindy has consistently sought to foster environments where others thrive.

Outside her professional pursuits, Cindy treasures her family role, finding joy in moments shared with her husband, Brian, and their family. In her downtime, she delights in walking their dog, exploring new places, and enjoying life's simple pleasures.

With a compassionate heart and diverse experience dedicated to service, Cindy is committed to making a positive impact on those around her, embodying the essence of leadership and coaching. Drawing from her background as a Professional Leadership Coach, Associate Certified Coach (ICF), and Strengths Champion Coach, she equips individuals and teams with the tools and insights needed to thrive in both their personal and professional lives.

> *"Whatever you do, work at it with all your heart, as working for the Lord, not for human masters"*
>
> – Colossians 3:23 (NIV)

"I'm so sorry to inform you that your son has died."

After receiving the devastating news of my son's unexpected passing, I found myself wrestling with deep grief and a sense of loss that seemed unbearable. In the midst of this struggle, I turned to my faith for peace and guidance, looking for strength in God, knowing that His plan would prevail. This experience changed how I would not only navigate personal challenges, but how I would approach leadership.

If it weren't for that tragedy, which changed the entire trajectory of my life, I might not have developed the deep conviction that I needed to share what I've learned and experienced along my journey. My faith in God provided hope amidst the pain, instilling in me the determination to persevere. As I continue to navigate through all kinds of turmoil and uncertainty, my faith remains steadfast, shaping every step of my journey in leading others.

Leading is difficult; it often requires courage and commitment. For those leaders who are people of faith, allowing your faith to play a central role in your leadership approach will help you find strength and receive sound guidance. When you lead others through faith, trusting in God's wisdom and plans, you act with hope and assurance, enabling you to create a workplace that works.

> *"'For I know the plans I have for you,' declares the Lord, 'plans to prosper you and not to harm you, plans to give you hope and a future.'"*
>
> — JEREMIAH 29:11 (NIV)

This transformative experience changed my leadership style and how I would approach coaching.

1. COACHING FOR LEADERSHIP GROWTH

Whether you coach others or you're receiving coaching, you can enhance a leader's personal development and leadership skills. In a coaching relationship, the leader receives feedback and encouragement to reach their goals while keeping their core values in mind. An additional benefit of coaching is that it allows clients to lead in collaborative settings with diverse individuals who bring their unique backgrounds, experiences, personalities, and strengths with them. Coaching can serve as a powerful tool for resolving conflicts that may arise because of diversity in individuals. A coach can assist you in examining the different skills you bring to the table or wish to improve, such as communication with others or gaining a better understanding of yourself. As a leader, you may encounter a myriad of challenges—as well as opportunities—for growth on any given day. A coach, a neutral third party, is genuinely invested in your success and provides invaluable support and guidance.

> *Whether you coach others or you're receiving coaching, you can enhance a leader's personal development and leadership skills.*

By investing in coaching, you set up yourself and your team to tackle challenges effectively and thrive in the modern work environment, fostering creativity and driving growth.

Whether you coach others or you're receiving coaching, you can enhance a leader's personal development and leadership skills.

Some of the basic techniques in coaching are active listening, posing powerful questions, creating space for verbal processing, and providing guidance on steps toward reaching established goals. There is great focus, intentionality, and purpose within a successful coaching partnership.

Additionally, there is such power in listening to others and hearing them. You want to know others are listening to you, and others hope for the same level of attention—this is a big part of receiving coaching. When you have this deep sense that you've been heard, you feel loved, accepted, and motivated to move forward.

When integrating your faith into coaching, you open yourself up to guidance from the Holy Spirit, enabling a deeper level of listening and understanding. Your faith can provide valuable insight, particularly in times when discernment or clarity is needed.

As a coach integrating faith, I have a valuable advantage: it's easier to discern what's not being said. This ability, combined with active listening, has proven transformative with my clients. When I ask powerful questions that encourage them to delve deeper into their self-awareness, it often leads to moments of revelation, resulting in significant progress.

During one coaching session, a client faced several barriers keeping them from making an important decision. Drawing upon my faith, I asked probing questions that highlighted the root of what was holding him back. Together, we identified the obstacles and prepared actionable steps to overcome them. Witnessing his transition from feeling stuck to confidently pursuing his purpose was quite fulfilling.

In my experience, clients' moments of reflection, or "aha!" moments, signify the profound impact of guidance infused with faith. These instances reaffirm the importance of integrating faith into coaching practices.

Improving as a leader begins with understanding yourself. Here are the key foundational elements that a coach may focus on to practice and embody faithful leadership:

1. **Identity** – Understanding who you are. Coaching can guide you on a self-discovery journey. This will help define some of your unique characteristics, which are a part of self-awareness. When you grasp your identity, your confidence increases and ultimately enhances the workplace.

2. **Core values** – Your most important beliefs and principles. They guide your decisions, including how you spend your time. Understanding your values fosters a culture where shared principles guide decisions.

3. **Beliefs** – Understanding your beliefs is key, particularly in the workplace. Clear beliefs enable you to comprehend your attitudes and actions, thereby inspiring a vision that spills over into the workspace.

4. **Strengths** – Identify your talents, abilities, and areas where you excel. Doing so helps your personal growth and success in various areas of life, including within the workplace. Recognizing workplace strengths can transform the organization, leading to greater productivity and collaboration as tasks and team members' skill sets align.

5. **Weaknesses** – They're not something to be ashamed of, nor should they be discouraging. Acknowledging them is crucial for growth. Donald Clifton, the developer of *Clifton-Strengths*, Gallup's online psychological assessment, suggests you learn to manage them instead of trying to fix them. Understanding how you manage your weaknesses improves teamwork.

6. **Passions** – What topics resonate with you and stir your heart? Understanding and working within your passions can bring you great personal fulfillment and foster a more engaged work team.

One client came to me as she was looking for a new job. She wasn't sure what direction she should take. Together, we explored her identity, values, beliefs, strengths, weaknesses, and passions. We broke down each of these areas, discussing her strengths and how she could specifically use them. Surprised by one of her top strengths, she learned what that meant and how to exercise it through the opportunities that were right in front of her. This strength became invaluable in her new endeavors.

Before our coaching sessions ended, she got a new position where she could use her strengths while holding on to her values and beliefs. Applying the coaching principles, she grew as a leader and cultivated a cohesive team. Empowered by her approach, the team surpassed previous sales records. This client praised her team and their accomplishments, while having a sense of leadership fulfillment.

Coaching rooted in faith prioritizes your overall well-being, acknowledging the significance of your physical, emotional, and spiritual needs. Recognizing the value of these aspects underscores the importance of addressing them for your success. A team of individuals whose overall well-being is a priority is well-supported.

Coaching was part of my life long before I was trained as a professional leadership coach. My years of working in the finance industry were a time to coach, encourage, and assist those who wanted to buy their first home, another home, or set them up in a better financial position. This involved finding out their hopes and dreams, helping them understand how to achieve them, and providing encouragement—as well as support—throughout the process.

My extensive involvement in ministry has also provided many opportunities for engaging in different forms of coaching. I receive deep satisfaction from cultivating meaningful relationships and encouraging individuals to explore and actively pursue their aspirations and ideas. There is a dream or an idea in each of our hearts and, sometimes, we just need someone to come alongside us, draw it out, and believe in us.

2. INTEGRATING FAITH IN TRAINING

Onboarding processes are an integral part of ensuring a successful start of any new role. Successful and confident employees can be attributed to an intentional onboarding experience. Approaching the onboarding process with a perspective grounded in faith can offer valuable insights into what truly matters. For individuals of faith, taking time to pray for guidance on how to approach the onboarding process and how the new employee will perceive it can be very beneficial. By seeking spiritual guidance, you can align your intentions with the principles of compassion, understanding, and service, fostering a welcoming and supportive environment for the new employee.

Before diving into the onboarding process, it's important to identify your key priorities. What needs to be focused on? The goal of onboarding is to benefit the new member and support their success. By prioritizing humility and serving others, you live out your faith in the workplace. This not only contributes to the individual's success but also leads to fostering an organizational culture built on shared beliefs and values.

> *"Do nothing out of selfish ambition or vain conceit. Rather, in humility value others above yourselves, not looking to your own interests but each of you to the interest of the others."*
>
> – PHILIPPIANS 2:3-4 (NIV)

The onboarding process should focus on the new employee's success, which will ultimately benefit the organization. You are establishing a new relationship, which requires time, trust, and authenticity. It is essential to communicate to the new employee that you value their input and that their voice matters within the organization.

Onboarding strategies:

1. Build rapport by getting to know the new employee.
2. Allocate time to interact with them regularly.
3. Ask open-ended questions for dialogue.
4. Promote idea sharing.
5. Offer words of encouragement and affirmation.

Implementing the above strategies contributes to the establishment of trust. As noted by Patrick Lencioni, an author focusing on team management, trust serves as a solid foundation for effective teamwork.

Onboarding objectives:

1. Understand the organization's values and goals.
2. Set clear expectations.
3. Learn specific procedures.
4. Prepare for the new role.

Leaders should take the initiative to support new employees, giving them clear guidance and answering questions proactively. It's essential that new employees clearly understand their role and how they fit within the organization. Leaders should provide a simple explanation of what the new employee's responsibilities will entail and how they contribute to the organization's mission, vision, and core values.

Onboarding key questions:

1. What are the responsibilities of the role, and what are the goals for the new employee?
2. What is expected of the employee at each stage?
3. Who will provide oversight and support?
4. Who should the employee contact for assistance or guidance?

New employees might not always know what to ask, so it's crucial for you to take a proactive approach in supporting them from the onset to set them up for success.

Investing time in genuinely understanding each new employee not only makes them feel valued, but also creates a sense of belonging within the organization. This, in turn, significantly enhances their performance in their respective roles. Effective onboarding, therefore, benefits not only the individual but also the organization at large, contributing to a positive work culture and overall success.

"Therefore encourage one another and build each other up, just as in fact you are doing."

– 1 Thessalonians 5:11 (NIV)

Self-awareness is all about understanding yourself and how you interact with others. When you include your faith, you see this through a different lens. Recognizing your unique character qualities, strengths, and areas for growth isn't just about personal development—it's about aligning your journey with the guiding principles of your faith. Have you taken time to think about why you act or speak in certain ways? Embracing self-awareness isn't merely a journey of self-discovery; it's an essential step in living out your faith authentically, as a leader.

As self-awareness deepens, it not only enriches our lives individually but also lays the foundation for faith-driven leadership. Faith-driven leadership values a supportive community, spiritual growth, and humility. It makes sure integrity is a priority in all decisions, fostering trust and confidence. By embracing self-awareness and intentional growth, you infuse your life with purpose and joy, embodying the transformative power of faith in action.

God created each of us with unique gifts, talents, passions, and life experiences. With this truth in mind, understanding how to put your uniqueness to best use becomes invaluable. The more you learn about yourself, the better you are at cultivating your relationships with family, coworkers, and personal friends.

Understanding yourself is key to navigating life effectively. It empowers you to communicate authentically and thrive in various aspects of life. Without self-awareness, you risk merely going through the motions, lacking depth and purpose. By delving into our inner workings, we unlock the potential to make a meaningful impact on others and, ultimately, transform our environments.

ONGOING TRAINING

Offering coaching, either in-house or outsourced, will boost team members' personal and professional development. This is an invaluable tool to incorporate into your ongoing training regimen.

When you encounter individuals lacking confidence or failing to deliver excellent customer service, this can be a reflection of the quality of their training and support. It's unfair to put the blame entirely on them when they haven't received proper guidance or coaching. Learning from mistakes can be important, but it shouldn't be the only method of learning. Taking a proactive approach by providing thorough training and support will prevent mistakes and ensure positive people interactions.

Encouraging continued growth involves facilitating access to various educational resources. It's essential to support individuals to expand their knowledge and develop new and existing skills continuously, which nurtures their vision and passion, propelling them forward in their journey.

Today, there are assessments designed to help you understand yourself better. Tools like the CliftonStrengths assessment help identify individual strengths. According to Gallup, when people know and use their strengths, they are more engaged at work, more productive, happier, and healthier. This helps team members gain self-awareness and how to leverage their strengths effectively.

It is easy to integrate the strengths assessment into coaching relationships. This process allows coaches to set clear goals and identify actionable steps.

Facilitating strengths-based workshops for teams is a key aspect of my business, and I find them engaging and very rewarding. These workshops focus on cultivating individual growth while enhancing team synergy. Each person on the team knowing what their strengths are and how to use them creates a dynamic team.

Each person on the team knowing what their strengths are and how to use them creates a dynamic team.

Each person on the team knowing what their strengths are and how to use them creates a dynamic team.

Cathy, an attendee of one of my strengths-based workshops, shared the benefit she received:

> *"The strengths-based workshop was very informative in helping me understand how God has wired me, and how I can use that to lead others. It was also very insightful to understand the unique strengths that are combined when you go through this process with a team that you are a part of. When individuals on a team are working from their strengths, it makes the whole team stronger."*

When unity is a part of the culture, everyone is more likely to build each other up.

> *"Let us therefore make every effort to do what leads to peace and to mutual edification."*
>
> – **Romans 14:19 (NIV)**

3. LEADING WITH YOUR FAITH

Equipping and empowering others as a leader means helping them grow in important areas. You need a clear vision, goals to reach, encouraging words of support, and accountability to keep you on track. Using your faith as a guiding principle can ultimately create a more fulfilling work environment, fostering an atmosphere of trust and respect.

The following elements will contribute to the success of your team:

1. **Vision** – A clear picture of the envisioned future. This helps determine the steps needed to achieve the shared goal.
2. **Goals** – Set specific, measurable goals, creating actionable steps.
3. **Encouragement** – Uplifting words, prayer, or Scripture shared.
4. **Accountability** – Holding yourself or others responsible for the commitment.

As you cultivate these essential elements within your team, remember the power that faith can have in your leadership role. There's always a story to share, a word of encouragement to offer, a verse of Scripture to impart, or a prayer to be uttered. These practices have the potential to be transformative in the workplace. Reflecting on your style of leadership, consider how your faith aligns with it. Imagine a workplace where genuine care for the success of others permeates every interaction. Such a vision can become a reality as you work towards equipping and empowering those within your sphere of influence.

"As iron sharpens iron, so one person sharpens another."

– **Proverbs 27:17 (NIV)**

Looking back, I am reminded of the powerful transformation that integrating faith into every aspect of life can bring. From the depths of tragedy, a strong conviction emerged to guide me through some of the deepest valleys of uncertainty and strife, shaping my path forward.

Your faith is a powerful tool that can sustain you in times of adversity, fostering meaningful change in the workplace and beyond. By tapping into your beliefs, you can create a workplace that is successful, infused with purpose and compassion. This can lead to a future where work is not solely about earning an income, but also brings about a profound impact on workplace culture and personal satisfaction.

In this chapter, we've delved into the transformative power of integrating faith into coaching, training, and leadership practices. Now, empowered with these insights, may you step boldly into your leadership role, knowing that your faith can guide you towards creating positive change and shaping a future filled with purpose and fulfillment.

"I can do all this through him who gives me strength."

– **Philippians 4:13 (NIV)**

CHAPTER 2

Putting Your Heart into Your Work: How to Invest in the Hearts of Others without Missing Your Own

Dana Grindal

Prayer Minister, Founder of Whitestone Ministries Intl

danagrindal.com

teachingfellowshipinstitute.org

fearlessandfreecommunity.com

linkedin.com/in/dana-grindal-910084277

What Dana loves to do most is empower clients to overcome mental, emotional, and spiritual obstacles in their work and personal lives. Most recently, Dana has partnered with His Whole House Ministries to co-lead an online teaching platform called the Teaching Fellowship Institute. This platform hosts mastery courses, resources, community groups, and a school of ministry to equip leaders with inner healing, spiritual health, leadership, trauma recovery, freedom from anxiety, suicide awareness and prevention, and personal growth.

Dana is the author of the #1 international bestselling books *Healing from the Heart* and *Ascend: Preparing for Your Ministry Mountain*. She hosts a biweekly podcast titled *Fearless and Free: Spirit, Soul, Body*, a place to join others on a spiritual journey to be all God has designed for them to be—fearless and free.

As founder of Whitestone Ministries, a nonprofit ministry for inner healing, Dana loves to teach others how to hear from God and have a deeper relationship with Him. She is passionate about prayer and has witnessed firsthand the transformation authentic prayer brings to individuals, marriages, families, businesses, churches, and communities.

• • •

There is an age-old story about a businessman who was traveling to a major city of trade. The distance was long and tiring. The rugged terrain made travel difficult. Because it was well-known that many wealthy people traveled that road, robbers would hide out in various places along the way, waiting for an opportunity to rob them of their garments and possessions. An isolated traveler was an easy target for them.

One day, while traveling on this road, the businessman saw a man lying on the roadside. He had been stripped, badly beaten, and left for dead. Others had passed by on the other side of the road, not wanting to get involved. As the businessman came closer to the wounded man, he saw he was still alive. The businessman felt compassion for him. He stopped and bandaged his wounds to the best of his ability. Then he journeyed with the wounded man to the nearest place where he could receive care. He paid upfront for immediate expenses for the man's recovery out of his own pocket, promising to return after his business to check on the man and to pay any additional expenses incurred. The story of this businessman has become world-famous. He is remembered not for his name, or even for his business, but for his character. Maybe you have heard of him? He is known as the "Good Samaritan."

The story of the Good Samaritan has been told for centuries around the world. It transcends nations, race, and socioeconomic status. To this day, it continues to be one of the most widely recognized stories by children and adults alike, standing as an example for success in business and in life. You can find this story in the Bible, where Jesus tells it in response to a challenge from the legal and religious experts of the day. They were looking for a loophole to attain success. Jesus gets to the heart of the matter by telling them the story of the Good Samaritan. Jesus tells this story as a parable, using everyday experiences to illustrate moral and spiritual truth. After all, a picture is worth a thousand words! And what a picture He gives.

This story contains key principles for success for leaders. In my own work with clients, businesses, and organizations, I have seen these principles applied with measurable growth and transformation. I have seen individuals overcome incredible life challenges with great success, and work cultures transformed to a high level of productivity, standing out in their industries as leaders and building strong communities in the process. Let's take a short journey together as we unpack these principles in the Good Samaritan leadership model.

THE GOOD SAMARITAN LEADERSHIP MODEL

The Good Samaritan is found in Luke 10:25-37. For our discussion, we will draw on the five key principles of the Good Samaritan that relate to leadership and how to apply these principles to your organization.

THE GOOD SAMARITAN LEADER DEMONSTRATES MORAL CHARACTER.

The Good Samaritan certainly is traveling. He is meant to be somewhere and has work to accomplish. People are expecting him. Yet he is provided with the opportunity to be interrupted from his agenda to help another person. A person he doesn't know. He could justify many reasons not to get involved, but because of the strength of his character, he could not just pass by the injured man. He could not make the excuse that someone else would do it. In fact, in this story, others *did* pass by, including two well-respected religious leaders who were unwilling to help. The Good Samaritan takes personal responsibility for the urgency of the need, and he responds.

Morals matter. Character matters. Who you are when no one is watching is just as important as who you are when they are watching. If your character is not one of integrity and authenticity, if you are not the same person at work as you are at home, at some point, you will be found out and relationships will be injured. When stress is high and the pressure is on, if you can still be the same moral person, you are a healthy leader.

As a leader, your heart matters. Your ability to connect to your own heart, to know yourself and your strengths and weaknesses, matters. Where you are strong and talented, you will excel. Life can look good on the outside. But those areas where you are not as strong or where you have unresolved wounds will have a negative effect on your relationships.

Increasingly in our culture, there has been a lack of parenting, creating a great need for coaching and mentoring in the workplace. God's design for the family was for it to be the place for young people to learn who they are and develop strong moral character under the loving and watchful eyes of parents. When parents are not available, or when they do not give loving guidance, young people can grow up learning to perform well to play a role in school or sports, but miss out on learning who they really are and why they matter. If they don't know their value as a person, it will be difficult to recognize or stand up for the value of others. Much of my work with individual clients is in this area of identity and character, helping them discover who they are and the value they bring to their work and world.

As a leader, your heart matters.

Application: It is important for leaders to have people in their lives with whom they can process their thoughts, feelings, and goals honestly. People that will ask the hard questions and hold them accountable. People that will support and help them with their strengths and weaknesses. That is the healthy way to work through struggles and pain as they arise.

Going Deeper:

1) Who are the one or two people in your life that you can count on to treat you with love and respect, yet hold you accountable for your responses?
2) Who are the one or two people you are helping to develop their character and whom you are serving as their accountability partner?

THE GOOD SAMARITAN LEADER SERVES.

In the telling of the story, the Good Samaritan has his own donkey. At that time, you were significantly wealthy if you could afford to own your own mode of transportation. The owner or master would ride on the animal. To walk alongside and lead someone else atop a donkey would place one in the role of a servant. The Good Samaritan is not concerned that others will look down on him for placing the man on his donkey and leading him to help. He is focused on the value of this other man's life, not on maintaining his pride or appearances.

A leader who is more concerned about looking good to others will, ironically, miss the heart of others. If getting the job done so they look successful is more important to them than how people are treated, that organization will struggle. They may draw talented people, but they won't stay long in that environment. When people feel valued and seen by their leader, they will feel connected to them and their organization. That connection will drive them to perform better with coworkers and with clients, resulting in a greater overall organizational performance.

Working hard and earning titles and accomplishments does have value. Individually, we should work to grow and strengthen the talents and experiences we have. However, we should also use those talents to grow and strengthen others around us. In that way, everyone benefits.

I'd like to share an example. John is an executive in a large corporation. He has had great success in his career. He works hard. He studies the markets and prepares daily for the work ahead. But he attributes his success to relationships. John values people. Whether they are coworkers, customers, bosses, political figures, or assistants, he is intentional in asking about their families, remembering personal details about them, and helping them whenever possible. He does not walk into the room expecting to be served, but instead, to serve. Having worked in the same industry for over thirty years, he would say his business is built on relationships and his opportunity to serve others.

Application: Leaders can make a difference in the lives of those they influence. Your words have weight. Your genuine interest in others makes a difference in them feeling valued. Making time to see them and know them, to serve them where you can, will empower their success—and yours.

Going Deeper:

1) How well do you know those for whom you work?
2) How well do you know those who work for you?

THE GOOD SAMARITAN LEADER HAS COMPASSION.

It is worth mentioning that, at this time, Jews and Samaritans hated each other. Seeing that the wounded man was a Jew would be reason enough, culturally, for a Samaritan to ignore him and keep going. The story is told that the Good Samaritan saw the wounded man and had compassion. He didn't see a label. He didn't see a race or nationality. He saw another person in need. He responded in the way any of us would hope he would if it were us lying there on the ground, left for dead.

I want to highlight the use of the word "wounded," here. In the original Greek, this word is "trauma." Trauma comes in many forms. Some forms are visible, as is the case in this story. Some are not as visible. We will interact with people in our work environments who are carrying varying degrees of trauma. They have been beaten down or wounded by life. These wounds, this trauma, becomes visible when they are triggered. We may be tempted to think that the wounded person is just being difficult, or "overly emotional," or overly shy, and want to respond by demanding that they respond differently. Broad statements and controlling responses like "just get over it" and "stop doing that" will further add to their wounds and not bring about the results you intend.

Let me give you an example of how this can look. C.C. was given a new employee to train. The business was fast-paced customer service. Whenever the young employee felt overwhelmed, she would freeze up. Instead of asking for help, she would just let the emails pile up unanswered. C.C. initially felt angry, thinking the young employee was being lazy, but instead of reacting angrily, she gave her a little space and was able to observe the pattern. When the employee felt overwhelmed, she felt unsafe and withdrew. C.C. is walking alongside the young employee to help her feel safe as she learns to navigate the new job.

People are wounded in relationships. We don't fully know what they have been through, or what they are working through outside of work. Pausing to see the person when they have a stronger-than-expected emotional response will give you an opportunity as a leader to make a significant difference in their work—and possibly their life.

Application: Taking that moment to connect and show compassion will go a long way in building relationships with the coworker, as well as helping them feel safe to share what is really happening with them. Then you can respond by helping connect them to the type of help they need to receive healing.

Going Deeper:

1) Can you think of a time when someone showed compassion to you? How did you feel?
2) Can you think of a time a coworker needed compassion? How did you respond?

THE GOOD SAMARITAN LEADER COMMUNICATES.

There was no 911 to call, or ambulance to pick him up. The Good Samaritan delivers the wounded man personally to the closest inn, where he can stay and recover. He cares for him himself the first day, then leaves to continue his business. He communicates to the innkeeper about the situation. He communicates his plans. He communicates expectations. He doesn't avoid the potentially difficult conversation with the innkeeper to convince him to care for the man. He doesn't avoid the potentially awkward conversation with the wounded man when he returns and finds out he is a Samaritan. He is open and honest about what needs to be done and sees it through.

Communication is key to success in work relationships. A good leader clearly communicates expectations and directions. Communication involves both listening and speaking. A good leader knows how to listen with full attention, make eye contact, and face the other person. A good leader knows how to communicate in a way that is respectful.

Communication styles vary based on people's personalities, as well as their family of origin. Individuals coming into a group setting will enter it while still in the emotional role they were in within their family of origin. Subconsciously, that is the way they learned to operate in a group, as the family is their first social group. The way people communicate in conflict may be very different from the way they normally would communicate, based on past trauma or family expectations. People who over-communicate, or under-communicate, are expressing a trauma response. For some employees, this may be an area where growth and training is needed. Providing tools and training for how to handle conflict can be very helpful and empowering to the group.

To illustrate how to help employees with this, consider Stacy's experience. Stacy was working as a risk manager in a large insurance company. She was transferred to the workers' comp department. The workers' comp department was a very negative environment at the time, the place everyone wanted to avoid and the place where it seemed careers would die. The work was difficult, and the morale was low—until Ray was hired.

Ray was the new manager over the department. Ray was positive and encouraging. He changed the department by genuinely caring for people. He communicated appreciation for their work. He communicated they were welcome and important to the company. He rallied them as a team. His affirming and inclusive leadership transformed the atmosphere of that department. The office even won awards for their performance. Turnover rates decreased dramatically. People wanted to go to work. They wanted to be part of his team. Stacy stayed for thirty years under his leadership. She has had many opportunities to bring this leadership into other work and ministry environments. Ray's ROI is continuing to bring high dividends.

Application: Offering a "lunch and learn" training by bringing in a motivational speaker or counselor, or hosting workshops facilitated by employees with strong, positive communication skills, can be an accessible way to teach. Mentoring one-on-one, or putting employees in mentoring groups, can also be a way to create a safe environment for individuals to overcome previous communication obstacles and feel that they are a valued part of the team.

Going Deeper:

1) How well do you communicate with others?
2) How well do you receive communication from others?

THE GOOD SAMARITAN LEADER IS GENEROUS.

Helping others is an investment. The Good Samaritan gave of his own resources. He gave of his time and energy. He gave of his money. To take the time to see the person, recognize what is needed, meet them in the moment, and see it through to a solution takes an investment of time, attention, and resources. The Good Samaritan models using his resources well. He models generosity, making room in his heart for others.

Investment is key to success in leadership. Invest in yourself. Recognize your strengths and seek opportunities to be challenged and stretched. Recognize your weaknesses. Being honest with your own heart about where you are opens the door to healing and growth. In those areas in which you are weaker, seek mentoring, training, or counseling, as best fits the need, and it will bring you the focused attention required for change.

Danielle learned the value of this from experience. Danielle works as a realtor in a competitive financial environment. Coming into the industry, she observed fairness expressed across all levels of experience and sales volume. She also observed how favoritism devastated team morale. Danielle was most impacted by the leadership of her first manager, who supported her and encouraged her not to give up when she first started. Her manager gave her the tools to become successful. She taught that success and timing is different for everyone, encouraging Danielle that if she did the work and used the tools, business would come. She now is called on to coach and mentor others in her office.

Invest in the people around you. Less experienced employees need encouragement and mentoring. Mature, experienced employees have wisdom and skills that others lack. Provide opportunities for mature employees to invest in others, either one-on-one or in groups. Provide coaching groups or workshops to share and strengthen work-related skills.

Application: Outside of the office, connect with your community. Offer a summer internship for local high school students. Create a scholarship program for a specific skill set that is needed in your industry. Serve together as a team to clean up a park, help build a playground, or pack meals for a homeless shelter.

Going Deeper:

1) What charitable or service institutions exist in your community (schools, shelters, daycares, elder care, animal shelter, etc)? What opportunities to serve are near your offices or meeting sites?

2) How can you make a positive impact on areas or people who have been beaten down by life?

CLOSING

Work is only a part of the journey of life. What you do at work, what is accomplished, will primarily stay there. But who you are, the lessons you learn, the character you develop, and the people you impact go with you. If you are a young leader still building your career, take the opportunity to apply these principles. Invest in them. The seeds you plant in your relationships will bear good fruit over time. Stay with them. If you are a seasoned leader, you have a wealth of wisdom and life experience. Look around for someone to invest in. What better legacy to leave than to invest in the people in your industry or community? Put your heart into your work, serving others generously, communicating compassionately, strengthening your own character, and building up others. You will be blessed!

Chapter 3

Will They Stay or Will They Go?: Recruiting and Retaining Talent through the Full Life Cycle of Employment

Cindy Schuler

Human Resources Consultant, Leadership Coach, Speaker, Facilitator

linkedin.com/in/cindys1

integristarhrconsulting.com

integristarhrconsulting.com/when-work-works

Cindy Schuler is a recognized human resources leader, author, speaker, facilitator, and leadership coach with more than twenty years of experience in the field. As the principal of IntegriStar HR Consulting, she provides clients with strategic direction in the areas of talent acquisition and retention, culture and engagement, and diversity, equity, and inclusion. Ms. Schuler also provides leadership coaching to established and aspiring leaders.

Cindy has published many articles and conducted training and development for many organizations, including the Society for Human Resource Management, Association of Legal Administrators, Business and Legal Reports, Pittsburgh Human Resources Association, HR.com, and HotelExecutive.com. She is a Professional in Human Resources (PHR), a SHRM Certified Professional (SHRM-CP), a Certified Professional Coach (CPC), an Energy Leadership Index Master Practitioner (ELI-MP), and a Certified Professional Resume Writer (CPRW). She also holds a certificate in diversity and inclusion from Cornell University.

Cindy is passionate about sharing her knowledge through speaking, writing, training, and coaching. She believes in trusted partnerships and assisting organizations in motivating their employees to perform at an optimal level.

If a healthy work environment where all applicants and employees feel valued and included is not the focus of an organization's recruiting and retention strategy, it will be difficult to retain talent and foster long-term success. Building and nurturing a healthy work environment is essential for recruiting and retaining top talent. It begins with the recruitment process and extends through the full life cycle of employment. Most importantly, processes and procedures must be audited and revised regularly.

Recruiting → Onboarding → Training & Development → Performance Management → Succession Planning/Termination

JANE'S STORY

Due to an increase in workload, a new position for an administrative assistant was created for an organization that had multiple offices across the United States. Jane was referred to the organization through a friend of a friend. No written job description for the position was shared with Jane, as she was told by the hiring manager that "the job description was in progress."

Jane was interviewed by two colleagues—one to whom she would be reporting directly. She did not meet any other managers or employees, although she would be required to interact with other employees across offices on a daily basis. An offer of employment was made that day, effective immediately. Jane accepted the verbal offer and started work the following Monday.

When Jane showed up to work on Monday, she was introduced to several people in the office whom she did not meet during her interview. There

was no formal orientation, and no introduction to department managers or others with whom she would be interacting daily in other offices.

Approximately one month into her tenure, Jane had a candid conversation with a stakeholder in another office in which she found fault with the process by which a decision was made. Unbeknownst to Jane, the stakeholder was a tenured executive who was a decision maker at the organization, and they were offended by Jane's criticism. Subsequently, Jane was counseled verbally and in writing for lack of emotional intelligence while speaking with a key stakeholder—one to whom she had never been introduced.

At the end of her second month of employment, Jane was counseled for lack of proficiency in utilizing Microsoft Office software. However, she was never told during the interview process that Microsoft office proficiency was required to succeed in the position, and she was not given an opportunity to attend internal or external training to improve her competency with the software suite.

At the end of her third month of employment, Jane was terminated for poor performance. Budget cuts prevented the department from hiring someone to replace Jane, and the other employees in the department were asked to shoulder the additional responsibility that Jane's termination created for the organization. While some of the tasks Jane had performed were covered by others in the department, other tasks fell through the cracks.

The organization missed several opportunities at each stage of Jane's employment. While it may sound basic, even rudimentary, the secret to recruiting and retaining top talent is creating and nurturing a healthy work environment for employees, beginning with the recruiting process. Anyone can sell a job, but it takes commitment and skill to build and maintain a healthy culture where employees will be motivated to engage and produce, which is a "win-win" for the employee and for the organization.

RECRUITING

The first step in building a healthy work environment is securing top talent for a new or open position through the recruiting process. A job description should be created and finalized before posting a position or interviewing any candidates for it. The job description should be error-free; everything from the formatting of the job description (fonts, underlining) to the type of bullets used (circles, squares, open circles, numbers, etc.) should be decided upon and in top form. Instructions on how to apply for the open position should be clear, such as providing a link at the end of the description, giving instructions about to whom or where they should send their cover letter and resume, and other such details. Referrals are wonderful, but the candidate pool should be open to allow for more than one applicant.

The application review process should also be quick and efficient. There are many people competing for jobs in the market, and multiple employers are competing to obtain that same talent. For example, recruiters can speed up this undertaking by separating resumes into piles of "yes," "no," or "maybe," allowing them to move quickly to get the "yes" applicants scheduled for a phone or in-person interview. That takes communication between recruiters and managers, as well as an understanding of why it is important to make quick selections for interviews and move through the process efficiently.

Applicant tracking systems are great for "weeding out" the applicants who do not qualify, but they do not allow for a potentially great candidate to explain their background, as they will have been eliminated by a computer system. What if there is an applicant reentering the job market with transferable skills and who is a star? What if there is an applicant who is moving from one industry to another and has transferable skills, but they are eliminated based upon having used the wrong keywords?

Another important factor in moving swiftly through the process is getting interviewers to give interview feedback right away. If possible, it is best to give that feedback on the same day of the interview. One or two days can make all the difference in whether or not an applicant accepts an offer from your organization or another organization. Organizations that show an applicant that they are willing to move quickly—even by making an "on the spot," conditional offer, pending a background and/or reference check—shows the candidate that the organization is interested enough in them to go the extra mile to secure their employment.

KEY TAKEAWAYS:

- *A job description for each open position at an organization is essential.*
- *Expectations and skill set needed to succeed should be clearly outlined in the job description.*
- *Consider the downside to applicant tracking systems and the number of applicants who may very well be qualified, but who do not get a chance to even compete because of mere keywords.*
- *It is imperative to move quickly through the interviewing process to secure top talent in a market where multiple employers are competing for the same ideal candidates.*
- *Consider making offers "on the spot" to a great candidate. It says something about how an organization operates, and candidates want to work for an organization that is "on the ball" and that moves quickly through the hiring process.*
- *Organizations that drag their feet, can't make decisions, and leave top talent waiting for feedback may lose that talent to another organization.*

ONBOARDING

After a candidate accepts an offer from an organization—whether it be verbal or written—the next step in nurturing a healthy work environment is making certain that the new employee has a thorough and inclusive onboarding experience. Time and time again, a new employee is onboarded at an organization with little or no direction. When an employee is not properly onboarded, there is room for error. For example, when a new employee is not introduced to key stakeholders, it can set the employee up for failure, as was the case for Jane. Jane never had a formal orientation and was not introduced to key stakeholders. Had she known that she was speaking to a key stakeholder, she may have made a different choice and not criticized a process by which a decision was made that led to her being counseled.

A poor onboarding process may also leave a bad taste in a new employee's mouth when they do not feel they have been set up for success. With so many organizations working a remote or hybrid schedule, it is imperative to onboard employees properly and to make sure they feel a sense of belonging from day one of their employment.

KEY TAKEAWAYS:

- *Onboarding an employee properly is critical to their success at the organization.*
- *Make certain to introduce a new employee to stakeholders and others with whom they will interact on a daily basis. Providing them with historical knowledge about the organization and an introduction to others by email or through a virtual platform is helpful.*
- *Connections and relationship building are essential to the success of the employee and an organization.*

TRAINING AND DEVELOPMENT

Training and development opportunities (internal and external) must be discussed during the interview process. However, if not discussed at that time, employees must be afforded the opportunity to learn and grow. Even if the organization is flat and there are no opportunities for a hierarchical promotion, there is always room for intellectual growth and lateral movement when an employee has reached their peak. For example, if a talented and loyal employee has been with an organization for five years and they have reached their capacity in their current position, managers must find a way to continue to grow the individual through personal development opportunities. If an organization does not have the budget to send an employee outside the workplace to acquire additional skills, there are other options, such as assigning an employee a mentor or providing the employee with an opportunity to gain skills internally that will allow them to move to another position or another department.

KEY TAKEAWAYS:

- *When organizations have a great talent who reaches their peak in a position, identifying growth opportunities is critical.*
- *Even if an opportunity exists in another department, identifying growth opportunities for employees will contribute to retaining top talent.*

PERFORMANCE MANAGEMENT

Managing employee performance starts the moment the employee begins their tenure with the organization. Check-ins should be conducted with new employees at the thirty-, sixty-, and ninety-day mark. Those check-ins should be substantive and meaningful. For example, at the thirty-day mark, a manager should meet with their new employees and ask for feedback about their onboarding experience. Some of the questions a manager should ask are:

1. How are you feeling about working with our organization after one month?
2. Were we clear in the interview process on the skills needed to succeed in the position?
3. Are we in alignment with respect to expectations and goals?
4. Did you meet key stakeholders and other department managers in other offices?
5. Is there anything we can improve in the onboarding process?

Those questions, phrased in a way that is relevant to the organization, can be used to be certain that manager and employee are on the same page after one month.

If expectations are not in alignment after one month, there is room to make adjustments. Likewise, if there are performance concerns at the thirty-day mark, expectations must be made clear, and a discussion regarding shortcomings should take place. The employee should be told that continuous and sustained improvement is expected and that there will be a follow-up between the thirty-day and sixty-day mark. The mistake some employers make is waiting to address performance concerns instead of addressing them in real-time. If the discussions occur, the employer has met their responsibility, and the employee has an opportunity to improve their performance.

When the sixty-day mark approaches, questions with respect to whether everyone is now in alignment, or still in alignment, should be asked again. By this time, the employee should be comfortable with some of the routine responsibilities of their role, and appropriate questions should be asked during a formal meeting between manager and employee, such as:

1. How are you feeling after two months of working with us?
2. Is the position/organization what you thought it would be based upon our discussions during the interview?
3. Are we now in alignment, after the adjustments we have made concerning "x?"
4. How can I assist with helping you be successful in your role?
5. Is there anything you would like to share with me?

If there were performance concerns at the thirty-day mark, a manager must ask if the appropriate resources were provided to allow for improvement and then provide feedback on the employee's performance since the last discussion. If there has not been any improvement in performance, the manager should advise their employee that employment could be terminated if there is no immediate improvement. Employers can give an additional month of time to an employee to improve at their discretion, but by the ninety-day mark, if an employee's performance has not improved, termination should be considered. In Jane's story, performance was discussed at the thirty-day mark and at the sixty-day mark, but no educational or coaching opportunities were provided before her termination.

KEY TAKEAWAYS:

- *Performance management is critical throughout an employee's tenure. It lets the employee know that their performance matters, and that someone is interested in their growth.*
- *Performance management provides an opportunity to improve upon deficiencies and to make certain that the employee's goals are in alignment with organizational goals.*

SUCCESSION PLANNING

Succession planning is crucial in an organization. Leaders should look to mentor junior level employees, download institutional wisdom and institutional knowledge, and provide opportunities to grow those junior level employees into leaders. Far too often, no succession planning is done, and when a senior level employee departs an organization, so too does the institutional knowledge. Preparing subordinates for leadership opportunities provides backup support if someone is out unexpectedly, provides senior level employees with an opportunity to take time off (i.e., create work/life balance), and it prepares the organization for a transition. And if, for some reason, an unexpected termination occurs at the senior level, if succession planning has been on the radar, there will always be someone who can step in and handle some of the tasks at hand. In Jane's story, she was only employed for ninety days, and because the department was not permitted to backfill her position, other employees were required to take on her responsibilities. Unfortunately, some things—things that only Jane knew—slipped through the cracks. This should never be the case. There should always be accessible documentation and someone—or several people—who can step in and assist with the tasks that need to be handled.

KEY TAKEAWAYS:

- *Mentoring subordinates is a privilege. Every effort to "grow" a subordinate should be embraced.*
- *Succession planning is important in any organization.*
- *Accessible documentation outlining key tasks should always be available to department managers.*

CONCLUSION

Will your organization be one that can recruit and retain talent through building and nurturing a healthy workplace? Will the organization's employees stay, or will they go? It depends on whether building and nurturing a healthy workplace is at the center of the organization's recruiting and retention strategy. Senior leaders must believe in and support the strategy. Supporting the strategy means supporting managers who lead departments and providing training on how to build and nurture a healthy environment.

Consider the audit checklist below:

- Job descriptions are drafted for all positions, formatted consistently, are clear and transparent, and have been proofed for errors.
- The application process is clear, the process is fair, and an applicant tracking system is not eliminating qualified candidates based on keywords.
- There is a comprehensive onboarding process where new hires are introduced to key stakeholders and understand the history of the organization.
- Performance management is an ongoing process. It is the process by which managers ensure that expectations are clear and employee goals are in alignment with organizational goals at the thirty-, sixty-, and ninety-day mark, as well as throughout an employee's tenure. If there are performance concerns, those concerns must be addressed in real-time and employees are given an opportunity and resources to improve on deficiencies.
- Succession planning exists so that nothing falls through the cracks when organizations are faced with a planned or unplanned departure.

This checklist provides a foundation for auditing the employee life cycle at each stage. If the checklist is complete and frequent audits of the processes and procedures are encouraged, it is likely that an organization will be able to build and nurture a healthy work environment where recruiting and retention are at the core of the organization's values. If nurturing that healthy environment is a core value, the organization has a greater chance of retaining top talent. More importantly, if an employee feels they are working in a healthy environment where they are able to learn and grow, the organization and the employee both reap the benefits. If there is a breakdown at any level of the employee life cycle, however, an organization risks losing or failing to attract top talent.

For more information and resources, please visit https://www.integristarhrconsulting.com/when-work-works.

CHAPTER 4

Lead Them Before They Leave *You*

Michele Fantt Harris
SHRM-SCP

Leadership and Career Coach

michele.harris19@gmail.com

linkedin.com/in/MicheleFanttHarris

Michele Fantt Harris is president of MFH Associates LLC, a leadership development and coaching services firm. As a seasoned HR professional, Michele works with organizations to create leadership development programs and coaching services to foster growth for their managers and future leaders. Her HR expertise has reached many industries, including education, nonprofits, healthcare, insurance, finance, and banking.

This is Michele's seventh professional anthology. Check out her previous books: *Humans@Work*, *You@Work*, *Imagination@Work*, and *Thriving Throughout Your Retirement Transition*.

Michele is a member of the International Coach Federation, a Certified Career Management Coach (CCMC) through the Academies, and a Certified Retirement Coach through Career Partners International.

Michele received her B.A. degree from the University of Maryland, Baltimore County, a Master's of Administrative Science from Johns Hopkins University, and her Juris Doctorate from the University of Baltimore School of Law.

Michele is an adjunct instructor at Catholic University and Prince George's Community College. She resides in the District of Columbia with her husband and their rescue canine.

• • •

Who would think a company loss could lead to one of its greatest employee retention tools? That is exactly what I witnessed at National Cooperative Bank.

During the Great Recession, the Bank experienced several reduction-in-forces with the loss of some key employees. Serving as the Executive Vice President in Human Resources, I suffered a major blow in the loss of my Learning and Development team. They had started a leadership development program, entitled "LEAD," that allowed participants to develop their leadership and management skills while working as a team to complete a capstone project for the organization.

In the Bank's efforts to eliminate many management layers in the organization, at the end of the recession, we had lost several key employees because of the RIFs. Also, other potential future managers and leaders left the Bank to move to other, potentially more "secure" industries. We found that the management layer under the executive team was not prepared for leadership roles, and future succession management vacancies would go to more experienced external candidates. The Bank needed to take action to grow the next layer of leadership.

If you have found yourself in a similar situation, where people need to learn and grow, even though times are tough and budgets are cut, consider adding a new professional development program.

That is how the Management at NCB program was born. I worked with outside consultants to develop a program to address the future strategic human capital needs of the Bank. We interviewed and got oral assessments of the future leadership development needs of the bank from each executive council member, including the CEO.

The senior leadership team identified the following content areas:

1. Coaching/Career Development – setting expectations, providing feedback, and leading the difficult conversations to drive strong performance at all levels on their teams.
2. Leadership – working from an enterprise mindset; taking ownership of results for the teams they lead and collaborating effectively with other bank departments and locations to reach common shared goals.
3. Influencing Skills – understanding different points of view and the interests of different stakeholders. Influencing others to reach sound decisions and actions. Resolving conflicts constructively.

It was a conscious decision to title the program "Managing at NCB" and not "Leading at NCB" at that time. Many of the participants had just been promoted to a manager level, which meant that they were leading a small team of people or managing a significant project for their team.

Persons promoted to a manager level do not automatically become a leader for the organization. William Arruda of Forbes Magazine cites these distinctions that set leaders apart from managers:

1. Leaders create a vision, managers create goals.
2. Leaders are agents of change, managers maintain the status quo.
3. Leaders take risks, managers control risks.
4. Leaders build relationships, managers build systems and processes.

Although some of our managers had management and leadership capabilities, the bank decided to start from the basic management premise. I polled all executive council members to identify individuals who would be future managers and leaders in the bank. We had to develop a program that would meet all participants where they were in their career and enhance their future development. We recognized that many of the participants had grown up in the Bank from a functional job to a managerial position, yet we had to develop many of the leadership skills for their future personal growth and development and the Bank's management succession. The bank needs management and leadership skills for the organization to thrive, and to meet the needs of the ever-changing business environment.

Growing managers or leaders is an ongoing process. We created a six-month program that began with managing and planning skills, progressively developing participants into managerial candidates who led and inspired their teams with vision. Luckily, our two consultants were expert trainers and facilitators. They worked with me to develop a learning program for participants' personal growth and development that would also lead to a strong management "bench" for the Bank's succession management.

The six-month program included a pre-assessment tool for participants and their managers, followed by four in-house training classes and participants' personal growth and development plans. Recognizing that each of our regions have a different culture and personality, we chose 360 degree assessment tools that capture the management competencies that would provide the knowledge, skills, and abilities to make the participant successful in their current role and prepare them for future growth within their region and in the Bank.

> *The point is not to become a leader. The point is to become yourself completely—all your skills, gifts, and energies—in order to make your vision manifest. You must, in sum, become the person you started out to be, and to enjoy the process of becoming.*
>
> — **WARREN BENNIS**

The Managing at NCB program included the following components that, together, created a strong and agile learning environment.

ASSESSMENTS

We used self- and 360 degree assessments to increase the participants' self-awareness about their strengths and weaknesses. The self-assessment generated an overall profile and helped each participant determine their competency areas and those which were in need of improvement. We used *The Leadership Circle 360 Profile (LCP)*. This tool measures leadership competencies, as well as behavior that supports or inhibits the development of leadership skills. The LCP provided a full picture of the data collected about the participant, who also gave and received valuable feedback from their supervisors, peers, and direct reports.

The 360 assessment tool is invaluable, as it lets participants know what is important to their manager and those they need to lead. It identifies strengths to build upon, highlights gaps in the participant's awareness, and reduces one's potential for derailment. It is essential to note that the 360 degree assessment tool was being used for the employee's personal and professional growth and development, <u>not</u> for performance evaluation purposes.

TRAINING

Four full-day training sessions provided structured content that explored key leadership skills and practices, as well as opportunities for participants to learn together with their colleagues. Topics for the training sessions included "Leading with Emotional Intelligence," "Effective Feedback and Communication," "Managing Conflict," "Influencing Stakeholders," "Building Sustainable Trust," "Employee Engagement," and other competency development skills.

Professional development studies show that color engages the senses and contributes to an effective, positive learning environment. We added color to our handouts and training tools (flip charts, markers, sticky notes, quiet toys). We limited the program to sixteen to eighteen managers, seating four to five participants per table to allow for collaboration and engagement.

Our training sessions provided a safe environment for learning—confidentiality was stressed. Anything discussed by participants in the session would not be shared with their managers or other senior leaders in the Bank. The facilitators stressed that the sole purpose of the training was to build participants' professional skills.

In particular, we emphasized group participation. Each manager brought relevant information to the training with their diverse backgrounds. Through sharing their personal experiences and collaboration, participants learned from each other and accepted responsibility for furthering their own growth and development.

PRACTICE AND APPLICATION

The 360 assessments, training sessions, and homework assignments provided opportunities to reinforce learning through application, experimentation, and reflection. Participants created individual personal development plans to enhance their skill level to be in alignment with specific competencies that the Bank considered valuable. The individual development plan identified additional training and development opportunities to help the participant maximize their abilities so they could perform at their full potential.

LEADERSHIP COACHING – THE SECRET INGREDIENT

A critical component of the Managing at NCB program was the leadership coaching. In addition to the facilitators, the Bank recruited professional external leadership coaches to support participants in applying and deepening their learning in the context of their specific needs, strengths, opportunities, and challenges. Leadership coaching increases the participants' accountability to follow through on their development plan in addition to supporting and reinforcing their learning.

The International Coaching Federation (ICF), the governing body for professional coaching, defines coaching as "partnering with clients in a thought-provoking and creative process that inspires them to maximize their personal and professional potential." When the coach partners with a participating client, they persuade and encourage the participant to use their strengths, values, experiences, and knowledge to solve problems and manage more effectively.

The leadership coach holds the participant's best interests in mind and builds a relationship based on trust. The leadership coach is an independent party who upholds confidentiality and does not report to human resources or the participant's manager.

The coach does not tell the participant how to handle a situation. The coach works with the participant to get them to expand their ways of thinking for personal and professional growth. When participants think and feel positively about themselves and their circumstances, they maximize their growth potential.

The Managing at NCB program provided participants with a monthly coaching session throughout the six-month program. Many participants found the coaching valuable and continued the leadership coaching after the program ended.

The coach asks powerful and provocative questions, listens intently, and serves as a sounding board for the participant. The coach helps the participant develop new perspectives, insights, and lessons that will impact the participants' actions and accomplishments.

Leadership coaching provides a safe and supportive, yet challenging, environment for participants. Leadership coaches provide a psychologically safe environment where participants' risk-taking is rewarding, rather than risky. The coach works with an open mind, is nonjudgmental, and supports the participant, but challenges them to evolve and flourish.

The coach lets the participant decide which goals to work on and how they will go about improving. They may challenge participants on how their personal agenda aligns with the organization's future goals, but coaches do not impose their own personal priorities on the relationship. Rather, the coach listens to the client, facilitates the client's learning, and recognizes the client's strengths to help foster self-awareness.

Participants can learn, grow, and change if they have the right set of experiences and are open to learning from them. The coach helps the participant reflect on past events and analyze what went well and what they can improve. With the experiential learning, training, assessments, and coaching, the participant will continue to improve long after the management program has ended.

Here are examples of how leadership coaching works. Both examples are from other organizations and are not examples from my coaching at NCB.

In *Imagination@Work*, I wrote about my coaching experience with a recruiter, and our discussion about her options for using her current skills to enhance and develop her career. She enjoyed recruiting because she worked with a diverse set of clients and enjoyed working for search firms, but she wanted to do more than be a corporate recruiter. I asked her, what does "more" look like? She talked about learning the recruiting business—understanding how the company works at every level. We discussed how she could learn the business: shadow the firm's operating officer, solicit a new business client for the firm and work with the client from beginning to the end of the search, represent the company at trade shows, attend recruiting conferences to learn how competing search firms operate, talk to the firm's CEO to see how he started the business, etc.

After we developed and discussed at least five options, we discussed what she could do immediately. She decided to talk to the firm's CEO to discuss her options, and then ask the CEO or COO whether she could shadow them on special assignments with new clients. She really enjoyed the firm where she was presently employed, but wanted to learn more about the operations side of the recruiting business. If she ends up enjoying the operations side as much as she enjoys the recruiting, she will expand her career horizons with the company.

Coaching can also help a manager with simple skill development, like changing one's company presence. A client's manager, colleagues, and employees perceived her as being very reserved and cold. She only interacted with her team at work, but rarely attended company events. As she moved up in the organization, she was expected to attend business meetings, including the board meetings. She talked about how she was very comfortable with her own team while they were at the office, but preferred not to socialize with her work colleagues outside of the work environment. She realized that she wanted to progress in her career at the organization and realized that attending board meetings was now a work expectation.

We explored her fears of attending outside company events. She did not attend the company holiday party and the cocktail hour before the board meeting because she did not drink alcohol. She feared what questions the board members would ask her about the organization. We talked about how she could take small steps and gradually work her way up to attending the full outside event. We discussed how she could read the CEO's summary and departmental summaries before each quarterly board meeting to be prepared to address issues that would be discussed. This would help increase her knowledge of other areas of the organization. She also studied the profile summaries of the board members so that she would be prepared to discuss something of interest with each member. She would attend the last portion of the cocktail hour and partner with another new manager at each board meeting. The more board meetings she attended, the more comfortable she became with unfamiliar work situations.

Although her issue is a very simple personal issue to overcome, she would certainly not discuss this personal issue with her manager. Leadership coaching is a valuable, confidential resource to help managers achieve their professional and personal goals. Coaching provides managers with an appreciative, empowering process that helps them overcome their fears and limitations.

Coaching was the "secret ingredient" in the Managing at NCB program. I wrote in *Imagination@Work*, "Coaching helps to change an employee's attitude or mindset, which is the one thing with which HR professionals and managers universally struggle. You know the adage, 'you can lead a horse to water but you can't make it drink?' Well, a good coach can get the horse to drink—can encourage and motivate the employee to change their behavior and their attitude. Coaching delves into the inner mind of your employees: their fears, anxieties, strengths, weaknesses, positive and negative feelings, and aspirations."

Leadership coaches are the important guides of the leadership development program who simply ask the participant questions and allow them to "unearth" what is hindering them from maximizing their full potential in their jobs, their work, and in their daily lives.

MEASURING THE SUCCESS OF THE PROGRAM

After the training, exercises, and coaching ended, there was still more to be done in the Managing at NCB program. The next step was to measure the program's success.

On the last official day of the program, we invited the participants, their managers, and the senior leaders of the organization to attend the graduation ceremony. We asked the participants to be prepared to reflect on their leadership goal that they identified at the beginning of the program. The CEO gave an inspiring talk about the value of their management skills to their professional development and the Bank's success. The program organizers gave each participant a certificate and took individual and group pictures. Human Resources placed an article in the company newsletter identifying the program graduates and included their group picture with the CEO. This communication increased the visibility of the program and increased the interest of future participants.

Good measurement tools will deliver key metrics about the program. To get the participants' reactions, we sent out post-program surveys to them. The survey also evaluated the program's implementation, its effects, and its long-term impact.

The program's success was an ongoing evaluation. I measured retention rates, promotion rates, and other key performance indicators. Over 80% of the program's graduates remained with the Bank and are still there presently, or stayed until their retirement. More than 95% of the graduates received a promotion to a higher level position or received an in-place promotion to an officer level position. One participant, from the 2016 graduating class, started the program as an Assistant Vice President and is now the Bank's Chief Information Officer and is a member of its executive council. Another participant, from the 2017 graduating class, started the program as a Vice President and is now the Bank's Chief Credit Officer, as well as also being a member of the executive council.

THE NEXT EVOLUTION

In 2023, the Managing at NCB program (MANCB) was revised to the Leading at NCB Program (LANCB). Those participants who completed the MANCB program prior to 2020 were invited to participate in the new program. After the pandemic, the Bank went through a major transition in its senior leadership team, gaining a new CEO, CFO, CHRO, and COO. Now, the program offers both virtual and in-person sessions and uses CliftonStrengths (formerly Strengths Finder) and DISC assessments.

The LANCB program added a practicum experience where participants will be assigned an organizational project to do collaboratively, their task being researching and developing a plan to solve the organizational issue. The project will be determined and administered internally by the Bank, with its findings being presented to the members of the executive council at the end of the program for their review and acceptance.

The practicum will include additional training in leading with strategic focus, managing change, and influencing for action. The practicum features more rigorous practice, application, and action learning, as well as the secret ingredient of leadership coaching.

Build on my lessons learned and determine the best assessment, training, coaching, and measurement for your professional development program. Make your program unique to your company to retain your best and brightest talent!

After my retirement from NCB, I have continued with the LANCB program as a leadership coach. I dedicate this chapter to Leslie Branson, EVP, Chief Human Resources Officer, Nancy Nowalk, Vice President of Organizational Development and Training, and Diahann Smith, Senior Vice President, Human Resources, for their continued support of the program and for allowing me the opportunity to continue to be involved as a leadership coach.

CHAPTER 5

Playing Nice in the Sandbox: Workplaces Function Best When Everyone on the Team Is Mindful, Has Healthy Boundaries, and Demonstrates Respect

Nicole Hollar

Empowerment and Wellness
Speaker | Coach | Author

nicolehollar.com

linktr.ee/nicolehollar

shorturl.at/mort4

shorturl.at/dowHV

Nicole Hollar is a dynamic speaker, coach, and advocate for personal growth and empowerment. Her Amazon bestselling book, *Feeling Stuck?: Empower Yourself to Live a Happier, More Fulfilling Life,* is modeled after one of her highly successful one-to-one coaching programs, while her *OWN IT Podcast* furthers her quest to encourage people to take charge of their life, own their stuff, and get out of their way.

With more than two decades of experience in wellness and personal development, Nicole inspires individuals to unlock their full potential and live as their authentic selves.

Drawing from her background in wellness, neuro-linguistic programming, and Mental and Emotional Release®, Nicole brings an insightful approach to her coaching. Her ability to connect with clients fosters trust and enables them to make meaningful breakthroughs in their lives.

As a sought-after speaker, Nicole captivates audiences with her engaging style and relatable stories. Whether delivering keynotes, leading workshops, or facilitating group discussions, she shares practical strategies and transformative insights that resonate with diverse audiences.

Learn more about Nicole's coaching, *OWN IT Podcast,* book her for speaking engagements, and find empowering resources at her website: www.nicolehollar.com.

You can find Nicole on TikTok, Instagram, Facebook, YouTube, Threads and LinkedIn: @nicolehollarcoaching

• • •

Workplaces function best when everyone on the team is mindful, has healthy boundaries, and demonstrates respect.

While speaking at a recruitment event for teenage athletes—their sport was basketball—I explained to them that the lessons they learn on the court would influence their lives. During that time, I commended them for being at the event and having a commitment to improving their skills as individuals and team players. Much like those teen athletes, you are also a player on a team at work. Who is relying on you to show up today? Who are you relying on?

During my talk, I told the audience that not every person in the room will be the high scorer, or the best ball handler, or have the expert vision to set up a play. Yet, they all had an important role, and each one, much like you, could not succeed without the rest of the team.

It's not just about showing up, however. It is about committing to being present, communicating your needs and being open to hearing those of others when you are on the court in the workplace.

As an empowerment and growth coach, I show people how capable they are and give them the necessary tools to evolve and grow. Recently, my *Breakthrough Coaching* client, Jessica, and I discussed a situation at work that often leaves her and her coworkers frustrated. She is not meeting timeline expectations, and her coworkers are not cooperating with her in a way that would help her meet the demands of her job. Jessica's role in marketing has her wearing many hats, keeping her busy moving about the office and attending virtual meetings in addition to creating actual marketing products.

The root of their collective problem was a combination of ineffective communication, lack of personal awareness and accountability, stubbornness, wasted time, and an absence of planning.

Jessica, who worked in an office for at least half of the week, often found herself in hallway conversations where people told her what they needed, or asked how a project was going, which she often could not give a status update about because it wasn't even in her queue. For Jessica, on-the-fly hallway conversations where coworkers advised her of their marketing needs were ineffective. For this reason, she would ask people to send her an email about what they needed so she could see it while at her computer, versus a passing conversation while walking down the hall, her mind cluttered and on her way elsewhere—often to meetings which she described as "a frequent waste of my time."

For teams to function best, individuals must have quality communication, know their roles, and be accountable for their actions.

They must also be mindful about what they really need from the people around them, and that their top priority may not be another person's.

COMMUNICATE LIKE A BENDY STRAW

To communicate your needs, it is great if you know how someone prefers to receive information so you can deliver it most effectively. Knowing how you learn is also important, so you can explain how you best receive information. Jessica, for example, knew she needed tasks written down and routinely asked for work requests in email form.

If you have an ongoing fight involving not remembering an important date, and you know you need it written down and not delivered in conversation on the fly, tell the person. Likewise, if someone wants to remember and has asked you to write it down, even if it is not what you need to recall an item, do it. Those are examples of behavioral flexibility.

KNOW YOUR LEARNING STYLE

There are four primary modes of learning: watching, listening, doing, and assimilating data. In school, many science or work-study programs utilize multiple learning methods. First, students learn in the classroom, usually by listening to the instructor and reading the material, followed by a hands-on practicum where they get to apply their skills.

Primary Modes of Learning

Visual (V): Seeing it or reading it.

Auditory (A): Listening to its explanation.

Kinesthetic (K): Doing it or being hands-on.

Auditory Digital (Ad): Getting all the data in various ways to assimilate.

When you listen to people speak, listen to the phrases they use. This will often give you an idea of their preferred learning method. "I love when people *tell me* about the specs on a car," or "*I read* about all the car specs online."

Imagine college students—some retain information best by *reading* the textbook, while others prefer only to attend the lecture and *listen* to capture the information. Yet another student may need to *re-write* all the information to capture it, and someone else may need to *teach it*. In order, these examples illustrate learners who are *visual, auditory, auditory digital,* and *kinesthetic*. Most people have two top learning preferences depending on the topic.

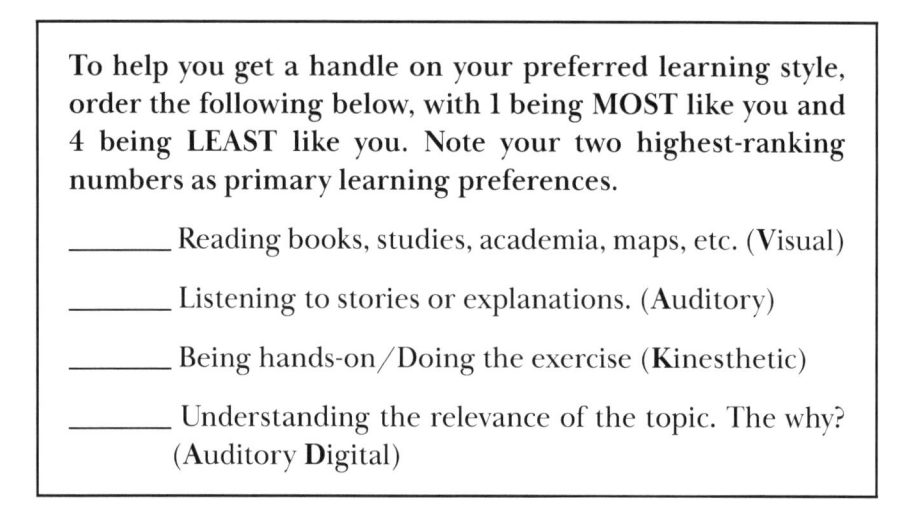

To help you get a handle on your preferred learning style, order the following below, with 1 being MOST like you and 4 being LEAST like you. Note your two highest-ranking numbers as primary learning preferences.

_____ Reading books, studies, academia, maps, etc. (**V**isual)

_____ Listening to stories or explanations. (**A**uditory)

_____ Being hands-on/Doing the exercise (**K**inesthetic)

_____ Understanding the relevance of the topic. The why? (**A**uditory **D**igital)

Knowing this information will allow you to properly communicate your needs and remind you to ask others how they prefer to receive the information you need to convey.

ASK FOR CLARITY

While some deliverables require a specific method or process, many do not. There will be times when someone may ask you for a deliverable or request something in a way that is not necessary for you, or not how you would do it. You get to decide whether yielding the end goal of the project or team is most important, or standing firm in your own methods is most important.

In the case of Jessica, who I mentioned earlier, she specifically and frequently asked people to communicate with her in written form, yet coworkers continued to tell her their needs during informal verbal conversations. It might not be what they needed, but it is what she needed. You can choose to be flexible in your delivery methods or not.

Empathy is an underused skill.

People are most successful and productive when communication is clear. Asking for clarity will help all parties involved be most successful and feel accomplished.

If you find that even after communicating your needs, you are not receiving information in your preferred learning style, what can you do to help yourself? In the case of Jessica, it was simple: she decided to carry an old-school notepad for people who were just not good at emailing. In her case, she knew that adding a task to her mobile device would likely result in her overlooking it. She was aware of who she was and her working style. So, she opted for a notepad because, to her, it symbolized work that needed to be done. Each day, she would transpose items to her master calendar. Jessica opted to contribute to the global goal instead of stubbornly insisting that if she didn't get an email, she wouldn't create the necessary marketing material.

I'M HERE, YOU'RE HERE

Whether you are in a hallway conversation, an important meeting, or feel trapped by a virtual "show and tell," focus on what is right in front of you. It is easy to become distracted by the environment you are in, or by the cascading thoughts and endless task lists running through your mind. But, because the brain takes in two million bits per second (bps), and our mind can only process 126 bps, you are wasting precious resources when you are distracted from the task at hand or the person in front of you.

To help you focus, imagine for a moment that you are in a movie dream sequence and everything outside of your immediate visual field falls away or into a blur. Give the speaker in front of you the courtesy you would want when delivering information, allowing other stuff to fade around you. Furthermore, don't distract other people who are trying to listen with sidebar chatter about its content, participants, the host, or another topic altogether.

You may find that by staying even fifty percent more present, the rest of what you want to accomplish in the day becomes easier because you are training your mind to stay focused and on task. Then, after the meeting, you can spend five to ten minutes with a coworker reviewing the positive takeaways or absurdities you just witnessed.

When I am speaking at organizations and the group is small enough, a tool I use to keep people engaged is asking intentional and planned questions. These questions can be used to confirm, clarify, or help shape the direction of the event. Periodic long pauses are another great way to engage people because they change the cadence of sound and break the rhythmic lull of continuous speaking.

MEETING THAT COULD HAVE BEEN AN EMAIL

How many meetings have you been in that really could have been emails? And how many emails have you received that did not need the "Reply All" button clicked? Before you schedule a meeting, there are some considerations that will make it more productive and its participants more focused and engaged.

Make meetings better and more productive with the following considerations:

1. Is it necessary?
   - Ask yourself, does everyone I am inviting really need to know the information I am sharing, or do I just want an audience?
   - Could I use feedback from everyone I am inviting?
   - Are there critical people I have left out?
   - Do Stacy and the other seventy people on this email chain need to know that I am attending Steve's meeting? Or can I save them from another "ding" and moment of unnecessary distraction by avoiding the "Reply All" button?

2. Have an agenda and set expectations for participants. Let them know why they are there.
   - I need you as a sounding board.
   - I am going to give you information to act on.
   - We are going to discuss a path towards...
   - Let's brainstorm ideas about...
   - I'd like to get your thoughts on/run by you...
   - We will decide...

3. Streamline the meeting to keep people focused.
   - Provide a brief outline.
   - Discuss high-priority items first.
   - Consider questions people may have and answer them as you go.
   - Hold off on taking additional questions from participants until the end.

4. Adapt the presentation to your audience without changing who you are.
   - Note whether you have a group that needs a slide deck to *see* or can just *listen*.

- Is it best if they *take notes* for future reference? Tell them.
- Would it benefit your meeting's goal to provide a bullet point summary of key takeaways for them to *assimilate?*

5. Participate if you have been asked to join the meeting.
   - Stay off your phone or computer for the purpose of looking up other things or catching up from the previous meeting that did not have your full attention.
   - Your full presence will improve comprehension and meeting speed because you are not asking the presenter to repeat themselves. Instead, you can ask questions or participate in a way that can expedite or enhance the meeting.

6. Set expectations.
   - Tell participants the next action item post-meeting and expected due dates, if any.
   - Likewise, if the due dates are not realistic, tell the meeting host promptly so reasonable adjustments can be made.

YOUR BOUNDARY OR MINE?

Learning to set boundaries requires an understanding of the entire situation and consideration for others. While boundary setting is you-centric, that doesn't mean that it's selfish. To have fluid relationships in any realm of life, empathy is necessary to create harmony. It's a moving dance involving stating your needs while respecting those of other people.

I DID THIS

Often, people create expectations for themselves that escalate, and they don't know how to get out of them. For example, answering work messages and emails at all hours is generally something self-created. The more it is done, the more people expect you to be on-demand. Or perhaps you have a growing amount of work meant for two people and the only way to complete it is by working longer and longer hours. If no one knows you are sinking—and even if they do, in some cases—there is little motivation to hire more people or redistribute the workload if possible. Then, one day, overworking finally burns you out or you become resentful. If being on-demand or having a seventy-hour workweek is an actual expectation of your company, ask yourself if you knew it from the outset and if it was within your boundaries then. If so, why is burning out okay?

BE MINDFUL

If you are someone who often sends stream-of-consciousness late-night emails, don't expect a reply until the next day. Your fire drill is not theirs. Yes, stuff happens at times. If you are someone who does this and didn't expect a reply, but you get one, remind the person that they are not obligated to violate their work-life boundary if they are doing so. Many people step over their personal line because of fear.

OPEN THE DANCE FLOOR

When discussing wellness with people, I often discover that many people do not snack during the day, something necessary to maintain glucose levels in the brain, alertness, and an elevated metabolism. Many people tell me that no one eats in a meeting, be it live or virtual, so they don't want to. I ask if it is an actual rule or just something you don't see. Then I remind them that someone needs to open the dance floor. When setting a boundary—like deciding you are going to eat your snacks, even during a meeting— you should still be courteous. Don't select smelly foods, like fish, or loud ones, like raw carrots; find something that will satisfy your needs and be mindful. Usually, once someone starts snacking during a meeting, others follow.

LEARN TO SHIFT

Whether boundary overreach is self-created or due to other circumstances, you have the right to set new ones at any time. For example, if you have allowed yourself to be the go-to person for everything in your department out of goodwill, allowing it to interfere with your actual job, you have the right to decline at any time. Honor that you have been a valuable resource for a long time, and remind people that they are resourceful enough to find an alternative solution, explaining that the extra work is interfering with your job performance. Just like values, boundaries may also change.

To help you become more productive at the beginning of each day, once you are at work (which might be at a designated workspace in your home), allocate twenty minutes to get a big-picture plan for your day or work on a pressing project. Once you've done that, check your emails and address other agenda items.

This new strategy may also mean sending people out of your office or going right to your desk without lingering. Most people report that it takes a couple of days for people to understand and accept that the first twenty minutes at work is your uninterrupted focus time. Here is your first chance to teach people your new boundary. Because people need to adapt to new boundaries, you must give them a little leeway to get used to your new ones.

REVIEW LIKE A FOOTBALL TEAM

Be like a football team that reviews each game so they can make needed adjustments as they go. They don't wait until the end of the season. Most people are subject to an annual review of some sort, often determining raises, bonuses, and promotions.

Don't wait for a year or more to receive a formal review or feedback. Seek feedback periodically from peers, supervisors, and subordinates, or give it to those same groups. Occasional constructive feedback gives a person an opportunity to improve, show interest in growth, get a boost of positive praise, and provides other people with the floor to air any concerns before they escalate.

STEP AWAY FROM THE CANVAS

Like an artist stepping back from his canvas to see the whole picture, every now and again, it is important to check in by stepping out. Look inward and ask yourself:

- Am I committing to being my best self?
- Can I improve how and when I communicate?
- Am I listening to what others are telling me?
- Am I focused?
- Does my contribution move the needle?
- Am I mindful that I am not the only person with needs and demands?
- Is there anything I can do to improve team unity or morale?
- What is bothering me, and is there a way I can address it appropriately?

The workplace is a social construct like any other, so it is important to recognize that you are a collection of people working independently and together to accomplish similar goals. By understanding and communicating your needs, creating and respecting boundaries, and engaging in quality feedback, the workplace becomes a better functioning, more respectful team environment.

Connect with Nicole

Learn. Grow. Inspire.®

To book Nicole Hollar for speaking events or learn more about Empowerment and Growth Coaching, visit: nicolehollar.com.

CHAPTER 6

Employee Resource Groups: Barriers and Improving Impact

Ralph de Chabert

linkedin.com/in/ralph-de-chabert-18b2055

facebook.com/ralph.dechabert

For over thirty-three years, Ralph has been partnering with organizations to produce lasting change in the diversity management field. As a consultant, he has worked from the outside across a broad spectrum of organizations—in both the public and private sectors—ranging from Fortune 500 companies to small nonprofits where he has collaborated in the design, development, and implementation of diversity and change management strategies.

As an internal employee executing change initiatives, Ralph has held various senior management positions, concluding as a senior vice president with global responsibilities for diversity and as president of the organization's Global Foundation.

Ralph believes there is greatness residing in each of us and every employee has the potential to make substantial contributions towards the achievement of organizational goals, particularly if and when they are valued. One way to help organizations maximize this employee potential is through the strategic creation of employee resource groups.

Ralph has a Master's degree in Education from John Carroll University, a Master's in Human Resources and Organizational Development from the University of San Francisco, and a Doctorate in Leadership from Spalding University. He is a Certified Executive Coach with additional certifications from MIT in Systems Thinking and Harvard in Labor Negotiations.

• • •

Within the context of a diversity management process, ERGs are intentionally created organizational subcultures, initiated by and composed of employees who have a shared affinity or identity and who coalesce around an intention to promote cultural change. Metaphorically, ERGs are like petri dishes, where individuals test and embrace opportunities to share cross-cultural identity experiences, resulting in mutual trust and transformative experiences. Members voluntarily give their time and discretionary efforts on top of an already demanding workweek to achieve the strategic intentions of the group, because they are inspired by a shared vision that is emotionally compelling.

More specifically, they are driven by the promise of systemic change, resulting in an increased sense of belonging, both of which are catalytic sources of meaning that propel their drive to create more inclusive workplaces and communities.

They drive change from the bottom up through grassroot initiatives, in collaboration with senior leaders who simultaneously drive change from the top down to strategically shift the culture.

THE BUSINESS CASE

Many organizations have diversity management initiatives with one or more ERGs in their strategic processes because of their potential to deliver some, if not all, of the following benefits, which typically align with strategic business goals:

- increased productivity and creativity
- supported personal and professional development

- increased employee engagement
- expanded internal professional networks, leading to increased workplace efficiency and effectiveness
- increased psychological safety, which supports a learning culture
- improved community outreach, particularly in the area of supplier diversity programs
- needed access to informal information, particularly as it relates to the unwritten rules in an organization
- supported recruiting efforts
- enhanced insights into diversity-related issues impacting the business
- engaged marketing resources in the development of multicultural marketing strategies

Considering their business alignments, ostensibly, ERGs should be fully integrated into the "business of the business." Unfortunately, it is not that simple, and, by drawing from my over thirty years of experience in the diversity space, I will briefly explore the reality surrounding the underutilization—lost potential—of the resources offered by ERGs and what can be done to make them more strategically impactful. Let's start with a retrospective look at the origin of ERGs and their related barriers.

HISTORICAL CONTEXT

Although it might sound trite and clichéd to say that culture trumps change, typically, it does. Given that ERGs are designed to effect culture change, their portfolio of initiatives constantly has them battling cultural headwinds designed to maintain the status quo.

One cultural inhibitor flows from the legacy issues associated with affirmative-action programs. In 1964, the US government passed civil rights legislation to combat rampant discrimination in workplaces based on race, sex, color, religion, and national origin. The legislation created Equal Employment Opportunity (EEO) laws to provide some guardrails against specific acts of workplace discrimination aimed at denying individuals opportunities to be hired and/or promoted because of their race, sex, color, religion and/or national origin. One tool used to comply with the law was the utilization of affirmative action, which supported equitable treatment of women and people of color during the hiring process and throughout their employment.

The tool was multifaceted and, when used correctly, should have supported a leveling of the playing field by ensuring that systematically marginalized individuals were given an equal opportunity to be hired and promoted. Further, the ongoing assumption was that once a person was hired, the field would be leveled and an individual's future growth would be predicated upon merit.

The assumptions, however, were flawed because they underestimated the strength of resistance that flowed from the cultural legacies of racism and sexism within organizations. The persistence of these biases is borne out in exercises I have conducted hundreds of times, with thousands of workers, in which two results have persisted: women are seen as not having leadership qualities to make tough decisions, and Blacks and Latinos are seen as unintelligent, which leaves each group struggling to receive leadership growth opportunities. These stereotypes become compounded for black women and are referred to as a "double bind."

These new hires experienced overt and covert acts of discrimination from those who wanted to maintain the demographic status quo, and as long as the hiring managers and organizational leaders did not manage the environment, women and people of color were set up to fail. These failures resulted in the "turnstile effect," where the new hires were exiting at rates equal to their hiring numbers. Under these circumstances, the concept of merit-based growth was fallacious at best.

I am reminded of a discussion I had with a manager who was not supportive of the efforts to bring women into the manufacturing facility. He would select the most attractive women and place them at the front of the production line, with no intention of doing anything other than "eyeballing" them, which is a form of sexual harassment that went unchecked.

When working in these environments, the new hires struggled because they were truly doing twice as much to be considered half as competent.

AFFINITY GROUPS AND EVOLUTION TO ERGS

While trying to overcome the barriers, women and people of color would meet, often outside of work, in like groups, to "pressure test" the experiences they were having in the workplace. These became "safe places" for "sanity check" discussions about their experiences. Composed of people with similar affinities, they were created exclusively out of a need for psychological safety and a need to validate or invalidate their experiences across their unifying identity. These were some of the early affinity groups that not only validated these negative experiences of those with similar identities, but were also places where members positively supported one another by sharing successful coping strategies. Furthermore, in this safe environment, if someone of a like affinity to the inquirer invalidated an experience, it was easier to believe than a dismissive response or denial expressed by someone who was not a part of the same identity group.

Eventually, groups became visible and passively supported inside their respective organizations. As they gained momentum, they held events intended for the group members and those with more than a passing interest in the group's activities. Generally, their activities were social, leaving them exposed to negative criticism, questioning their relative value to the organization.

Eventually, affinity groups morphed into a more formal structure, becoming employee resource groups, or, as some are more recently called, business resource groups (BRGs). They were designed, developed, and implemented by and for their specific identity or affinity group, with a major difference from affinity groups being that they are open to anyone with a desire to learn and grow from their membership experiences. Additionally, unlike affinity groups, ERGs are formally sanctioned by the organization. However, many of the negative legacies persisted and created headwinds against which they continued to struggle.

MIDDLE MANAGER BARRIERS

Despite tying their vision and mission to the larger organization's strategic initiatives and values, ERGs were, and frequently are, hamstrung by a lack of time, money, and people needed to increase their effectiveness. The sources of this lack of support were varied, and it was particularly disappointing when the support did not come from middle managers. Often, middle managers struggled with supporting ERGs because they had to prioritize competing organizational imperatives from executive leaders, and, when forced to choose, managers were inclined to focus more on those priorities with the most measurable attention from their supervisors. The pejorative descriptor for this is "the frozen middle." I am more inclined to call it "the conflicted middle" because managers might recognize the potential value of ERGs, but they ultimately prioritize the work that their senior managers evaluate and reward them for doing.

On the other hand, some managers were not supportive because they were not willing to change their attitudes and discriminatory behaviors around the value that women and people of color might bring to an organization. Operating out of a scarcity mentality, they resisted change in favor of maintaining the status quo because their dominant group's privileges were being threatened.

An example of this mentality occurred during a conversation I had with a senior leader in a distribution company about his unwillingness to support the ERG's call for improving the company's supplier diversity spend with historically disadvantaged providers. He refused to entertain new providers because he had good working relationships with the existing ones, all of whom were white and male. Because of his biases, he summarily discounted the well-researched benefit projections from the Black ERG, which outlined potential savings due to increases in competition, as well as greater creativity and possible introductions into new markets. If he was going to change, he wanted a directive from the executive team.

In a subsequent meeting, looking directly in my eyes, he asked the following question with a smile on his face: "When are all the white guys going to get their turn?" His comments were in response to executive leadership's directive that he strive to meet specific conservative spend requirements, stretched over ten years, which would have grown their spend with historically disenfranchised suppliers from one-tenth of one percent to sixteen percent, leaving white male suppliers with eighty-four percent of the spend.

That was not enough for him. The idea that this ERG had the attention of executives and that he was being compelled to give these suppliers, whom he presumed to be incompetent, an opportunity to compete for the company's business was a complete anathema to him. Shortly afterwards, he took an early retirement because "he didn't feel like it was his company anymore."

This manager's biases had negative ramifications on three levels: they overtly denied organizations run by people of color opportunities to compete for the business; sub-optimized potential success opportunities for his company; and knowingly or unknowingly manifested his biases about the capabilities of people of color within the organization at large and in their related ERGs.

Building on this issue of constraints and manager interactions, one of the largest problem areas for employees who want to participate in an ERG is a result of having unsupportive managers. Even though the employees are doing this work on a volunteer basis, in addition to all of their other work, it can be difficult to get managerial support. Frequently, ERG participants have shared that they overheard a manager saying to another manager that if employees have all this extra time for ERG "activity," then they must not have enough work to do. This kind of comment damages the psychological safety of an employee who has a desire to participate in an ERG. It also becomes difficult to perform at a high level if the employee does not feel trusted.

ACTS OF COURAGE

Apart from the tenacity related to overcoming constraints, those working in ERGs demonstrate courage and risk-taking in a myriad of ways, some of which are underestimated. Speaking truth to power in the presence of senior leaders is not always psychologically safe, especially when those individuals can make or break a person's career. Courage is also manifested in training sessions when members opt to teach others from a different identity through the prism of the group member's life experiences, sharing what it means to be a member of that identity both during and outside of work. Such sharing requires a willingness to be vulnerable, exposing the members to the possibility that what they share might be discounted or trivialized. This demonstration of courage also pertains to the senior executive sponsors of a given ERG. They, too, must worry about how they are being perceived by members of the group, as well as members outside of the group, as they express their own vulnerabilities.

CREATIVITY

Organizations can be parochial about their sources for creative inputs, excluding those outside of the function, believing outsiders might not have the requisite experiences to offer insights to improve products or processes. Here are some examples to the contrary:

- A group initiated a twenty-four hour hackathon, globally, among their group members, to provide potential solutions to four business problems.
- A Latin group initiated a program substantially increasing Latin accounts in a bank.
- A group with no sales, marketing, or consumer insights experience developed a novel niche marketing plan, which netted a consumer conversion rate of 18% vs the benchmark average between 12%-20%.
- A non-drinkers ERG in a beverage alcohol company created a unique space for non-drinkers to be seen and accepted, which helped the organization attract and retain non-drinkers, who make up one third of American society. Further, intentionally or unintentionally, they positively influenced the conversation among drinkers about their relationships with alcohol in the workplace.

It isn't enough to call them business resource groups. Organizations have to want their creative output. A limiting bias around the best sources of ideas maximizes the probability that potential contributions will be lost. You never know where the next best idea may come from.

IMPROVING IMPACT

Make ERG work part of "the business of the business," as opposed to being an ancillary activity on top of 100% of a member's other workplace responsibilities.

If strategic diversity management and the related ERG outcomes are critical enablers for achieving organizational objectives, then ERG members are engaging in "the business of the business" while executing against the ERG strategies. However, ERG members talk about "doing their day job" when referring to the work they get paid to perform and describe their volunteer ERG work as something that is seen as "non-essential" or "extracurricular" by managers.

If ERG work is part of "the business of the business," then organizations should give those in ERG leadership roles the opportunity to allocate a percentage of their paid work time, as one of their key performance objectives. I only know of one organization where the senior executives declared that anyone involved in an ERG leadership role could allocate up to 15% of their paid time to their work as a leader of an ERG. Further, they declared that anyone in an ERG committee leadership role could allocate up to 5% of their paid time to the leadership of the committee.

Organizations adopting this posture understand that to the extent ERGs potentially impact engagement, productivity, and creativity, their work is a business imperative tied to market cap valuation as well as the S (social) initiatives in the ESG valuation by large investors.

EXECUTIVE LEADER ENGAGEMENT

All executives should have multiple opportunities to sponsor different ERGs to increase the executive's multicultural competencies. Effective sponsors manage their need for centrality while listening, learning, and living—not leaning—into the various

ERG cultures. "Living" into the respective culture provides the executive with opportunities to internalize the experiences shared about what it means to be a member of that group's identity, both in and outside of work.

These executives also are conduits to senior leadership and are crucial to pushing change from the top down into the organization, while ERGs push change from the bottom up, creating this press towards thawing the conflicted middle.

ACTIVITIES VERSUS MEASURABLE OUTCOMES

To make their value proposition a reality with every activity, ERG members should ask themselves what the short-, mid, or long-term goals or outcomes of this activity are. These goals or outcomes can be qualitative and/or quantitative, and should be tied to the organization's strategic imperatives. This is crucial because senior leaders want to know if these groups are making a difference.

The answers should be fact-based and data-driven, where possible. Not having this rigorous accountability system leaves the ERGs vulnerable in organizations where external and internal cultures frequently continue to suboptimize their efforts. If the full contribution of ERGs is to be realized, they need to be radical in their efforts to be accountable for driving change within the organization by employing logic models which are populated by short-, mid-, and long-term measurable outcomes tied to strategic imperatives.

AVOID THE BINARY—IT IS BOTH/AND

ERGs should have both internal and external focus areas that are tied to the organization's efforts to achieve strategic imperatives.

To maximize opportunities for success, don't limit ERGs solely to internal engagements. Nor should they be criticized for internal efforts, because such efforts lead to a higher sense of belonging and increased engagement among the members. They also create a heightened cultural awareness within the organization.

An external focus allows the ERG to potentially make measurable contributions to an organization's goods and services.

THAWING THE FROZEN OR CONFLICTED MIDDLE

Senior leaders who function as executive sponsors of an ERG make it safe for employees to engage in them by having direct contact with the participants' manager. The executive can express support for the ERG members' work on both fronts, and can encourage the manager to build their subordinates' ERG goals into one of their performance objectives for the year. Doing so creates a dual accountability system by engaging the manager in the change process.

ASK THE QUESTION

Employee engagement is critical to organizational performance and engagement survey results should be disaggregated by ERG participation and location. One organization I am familiar with conducted a disaggregation study and found that ERG members were 5% more engaged than any other engagement scores, and in another year, their scores were 3% higher. If scores are low, ask yourself, "What needs to happen to make improvements?" If high, ask how they are able to achieve high levels of engagement while often being stretched thin, doing their paid job combined with the demands of their ERG work. Hint– consider replicating what it takes to gain true emotional commitment to a shared vision.

REWARDS AND RECOGNITION ARE CRUCIAL

For many ERG members, the reward is in the work's impact, but never overlook the value of rewards and recognition. Part of that recognition arises when acknowledging that leading an ERG is a challenging, resource-constrained management experience where the volunteers can leave at any time. Without formal member performance accountability systems, the successful ERG leader understands that the most powerful tool they have is the ability to influence the members to achieve business outcomes by keeping them inspired to achieve their shared vision.

GETTING WHAT YOU EXPECT

Finally, in workplaces that work, we believe that not a single one of us is as smart as *all* of us, and we know that ERGs are conduits to increased engagement, creativity, and productivity from which ripples of cultural change can flow.

Chapter 7

Creating a Jerk-Free Workplace through Courage

Eric L. Williamson

Consultant, Speaker, Jerk Expert

tailoredtrainingsolutions.com

linkedin.com/in/eric-williamson-57976b9

twitter.com/TTS_Williamson

Conflict resolution expert, business coach, and keynote speaker Eric Williamson shares with listeners that no matter how talented or experienced, and no matter what role we serve or title we carry, our success is not measured based on the work we produce—it is measured based on the relationships we build. He works with organizations to mitigate workplace friction by building stronger, more collaborative workplace relationships.

Eric is also known for being an expert jerk who turned jerk-expert. He is the author of *How to Work with Jerks: Getting Stuff Done with People You Can't Stand*. This book provides a strategy for working with jerks and building stronger workplace relationships.

Small-, mid-, and large-scale companies have partnered with Eric when they want to increase retention, improve performance, boost engagement, and promote a jerk-free workplace.

Eric is known as the "Connector" for making his message resonate with groups. He received national attention in NBC, ABC, FOX, and CBS News for his expertise in leadership development, stating, *"Emotional Intelligence (EQ) is the key component of being a successful leader; and is the most important skill that will help you thrive in today's ever-changing business environment."*

• • •

"Eric, this isn't what I thought success would look like."

These were the words that a worried and confused owner of a growing multimillion-dollar company told me right after I delivered my "How to Work with Jerks" keynote to a packed room at a conference out west.

He went on to say, "Eric, I don't think I'm a jerk, but I'm concerned my workplace is full of them—and I don't know what to do. Can you help?"

"Although my company had a record year in profits, workplace morale is at an all-time low. There is tremendous friction occurring between my customer service and sales team, and it's reaching a boiling point. The sales team raked in record profits last year and they are the engine that's driving the business. They are very demanding. They are rude, sarcastic, and usually treat their clients with more respect and dignity than their coworkers on the customer service team, especially when things don't go as expected—even when the situation is out of their control."

"As a result, the customer service team feels like they are being bullied. Some have developed imposter syndrome and have begun doubting themselves and their abilities to do their job. Some have developed emotional scars that are hard to repair. The situation is so severe that some customer service team members quit. I don't know what to do. I fear that if I reprimand the sales team, they may decide to leave, causing profits to plummet. But, if I can't gct this fixed now, it will have long-term, devastating consequences for my company. Not only will the low morale spread across the company, it may cause other people to leave also—severely jeopardizing profits and growth potential."

Sadly, this is what happens when "successful" business leaders don't address jerkish behavior. It festers and spreads through osmosis until it becomes a toxic, undesirable place to work.

What do you do when you have high-performing jerks who are great at their job and make the company a whole bunch of money, but leave a trail of chaos and friction in their path? Do you avoid the situation or do something about it? Based on my experience as a conflict management expert who specializes in the arena of removing workplace friction, ignoring this behavior makes a bad situation worse, and it's hard to recover. Instead, leaders must address jerkish behavior immediately before it's too late. Creating a jerk-free workplace takes courageous leaders. You must stand up to jerks and show them that their behavior is unacceptable. Equally important, you must also have the courage to face the hard truth: that it's quite possible that *you* are a jerk and must improve your behavior.

In this chapter, you'll learn some valuable strategies for creating a jerk-free environment through courageous leadership. You'll also learn how to have courage and why courage is necessary to create a jerk-free workplace. We'll examine the behaviors of courageous leaders, the challenges they face to create a jerk-free workplace, and why it's important to create one.

Jerk Definition Jerk /jərk/ *noun*

In my book, *How to Work with Jerks*, I define a jerk as "someone who doesn't use social skills as a necessary job skill. They create a toxic workplace, ruin relationships, and create unnecessary workplace conflict."

WHAT'S SO HARD ABOUT CREATING A JERK-FREE WORKPLACE?

Creating a jerk-free workplace is hard because employees' and leaders' social skills have eroded. People have been isolated for years and have had very limited, if any, face-to-face interactions with others. We forgot what it was like to be connected with one another. Furthermore, since employees and leaders don't have adequate training on social skills, they are unequipped to properly manage conflict or build relationships.

According to a 2022 Gartner survey, 51% of Gen Z employees are not prepared to enter the workforce because they don't have the proper social skills to interact with anyone or do their job. However, the erosion of social skills is not just a Gen Z issue: everyone's social skills have eroded since the pandemic. As a result, this has created incompetent leaders who can't lead or manage jerks.

Creating a jerk-free workplace is also hard due to limited resources and lack of self-care. Today's workplace is filled with stress. People are overwhelmed due to the increasing workloads, higher demands, and fewer resources. They are overworked and burnt out. Based on my experience working with various organizations to mitigate workplace friction, employees can spend up to three to five hours per week dealing with conflict from jerks instead of getting any work done. This is taxing on their minds and bodies. Employees seldom focus on self-care and don't know how to cope with stress. In the workplace, they get overwhelmed and, when they leave, they take it out on the people that love them the most.

WHY IS IT IMPORTANT TO CREATE A JERK-FREE WORKPLACE?

It helps retain and attract talented employees. Retaining talented employees continues to be a significant challenge. Employees have more flexibility and freedom to find jobs that align with their needs and values than ever and are more than willing to leave when their needs aren't met. As a result, employers have struggled to retain them. Employees are more likely to stay at a place that is committed to their well-being and supports their needs. When employees enjoy working with their peers and their leaders, they are more likely to stay, even if the position doesn't pay as much as other jobs. A jerk-free workplace yields bottom-line results. It increases revenue, improves productivity, and boosts performance and morale.

WHY IS COURAGE NECESSARY?

If leaders don't have the courage to stand up to jerks, then who will? Lacking the courage invites jerks to roam free and create a toxic and chaotic workplace. Leadership's responsibility is to set the tone and lead by example. It starts with being a model of good behavior who cultivates an environment of respect, harmony, and civility. This will inspire others to follow their lead.

WHAT BEHAVIORS MUST LEADERS EXHIBIT TO BE COURAGEOUS?

Leaders must be authentic, self-aware, and empathetic. You must be willing to display your vulnerability and acknowledge your mistakes and limitations. You must "prevent your ego from becoming your amigo." Leaders must understand that it's okay to make mistakes. It's okay to not have all the answers. This type of vulnerability creates a safe environment where employees feel comfortable being themselves.

WHAT ARE SOME WAYS TO HAVE COURAGE?

Leaders must stand up to jerks—period. This can be an uncomfortable situation, especially when business leaders are not used to standing up to jerks. Most would rather avoid the situation altogether than do something about it, especially when you don't know how to do it or what to do about it. Some walk on eggshells because they don't want to upset a high-performing jerk. However, part of a leader's responsibility is to address tensions before they escalate instead of sweeping it under the rug. Leaders must have tough conversations and let jerks know their behavior is not tolerated. You must grab the bull by the horns and face it head on.

Leaders must shield their team from other jerks or bullies in leadership positions who use their title and power to take advantage of employees. Protecting your team from jerks is a sign of a good culture, motivating your people to also protect one another from that intolerable behavior.

BELOW ARE SOME STRATEGIES FOR CREATING A JERK-FREE WORKPLACE.

HOW CAN LEADERS PROMOTE A JERK-FREE ENVIRONMENT?

Improve the culture through intentional connections. When jerks take over a workplace, employees get frustrated to the point where they shut down. They stop participating in meetings or discussions. They become quiet quitters. They no longer share ideas because they are disengaged. Instead of interacting with others face-to-face, they hide behind emails because they want to limit as much interaction as possible with that jerk. As a result, the workplace suffers. The workplace no longer receives the best efforts and ideas from their employees. According to Gallup's "State of the Global Workplace," published in January 2024, 85% of employees "Are Not Engaged in the Workplace." So, what can you do to boost engagement?

Leaders need to build intentional connections with their employees. Unlike mandatory interactions, where employees are forced to participate in planned activities, intentional connections are genuine, meaningful interactions where people are curious about learning about one another. You have an opportunity to learn one another's communication and working styles. A great way to build intentional connections is through authentic collaboration, such as working together on special projects or new initiatives. Through these authentic engagements, you have the opportunity to learn about each other's role and job demands and develop an additional set of skills. Team building activities that align with team interests and shared goals also are great ways to naturally build intentional connections.

When I deliver my "How to Work with Jerks" programs to organizations, one of the first activities I have employees and leaders do is a core values exercise. This activity helps employees and leaders understand what they value and why. They have better insight into what compels them to act the way they do in various conflict situations, a more in-depth understanding of their working style, and a greater perspective on how they handle difficult situations. This activity creates an environment of trust, respect, and engagement because they get to learn more about their peers and what is important to them.

A 2022 Gartner survey of nearly 3,500 employees found that when organizations help employees build connections intentionally, their employees are five times as likely to be on a high-performing team and twelve times as likely to feel connected to their colleagues.

LISTEN, UNDERSTAND, AND VALIDATE (LUV).

Another effective way that leaders can courageously create a jerk-free environment is through LUV—Listen, Understand, and Validate. Specifically, you must listen, understand, and validate their needs. When employees feel as though their leaders are listening to them, understanding their concerns, and validating their ideas, it sends a message that they are valued—that leaders truly care, are incredibly curious about their well-being, and are committed to supporting them. When employees feel that they have the support of their leaders, they are more likely to improve their performance, stay at the company, and continue to add value. Leaders can implement the LUV method in various ways in the workplace, such as through active listening and by being incredibly curious. Employees can employ the LUV method when they are interacting with different teams or stakeholders. For example, IT and business stakeholders work on similar projects but often experience friction. Practicing the LUV method helps build relationships so that they can mitigate the friction and work together more cohesively.

EMPOWER, DON'T MICROMANAGE.

Leaders, don't let your ego become your amigo. You must be okay with your employees being smarter than you. And you must trust that they can get the job done just as effectively, if not better than you—but in their own way! Stop micromanaging. Giving them latitude is gratitude. Empowering them to get the work done instead of leading every detail of the assignment will go a long way. It builds trust, respect, and accountability. People will be more engaged and more willing to participate in work activities.

TRAINING.

Leaders sometimes make a wise choice to fire jerks, but they inadvertently end up hiring another jerk to replace them. Why? Because you don't know how to assess or address jerk behavior. It may appear to be easier to get rid of jerks than learn how to manage them. If you never figure it out, you may continually perpetuate this vicious and pervasive cycle of hiring and firing jerks. It's an expensive and inefficient way of managing resources. A more efficient way of handling this is to have the courage to deal with the behavior by coaching, training, and managing them.

Creating a jerk-free environment is a skill as much as it is an intent. This means that leaders must have the necessary tools to manage conflict situations effectively and efficiently. When we are dealing with conflict, we have an opportunity to discover, assess, and leverage multiple conflict styles to mitigate conflict and defuse tense situations. Often, we have our own habitual ways of managing conflict. It's not always the best solution, because this can make a bad situation worse. Instead of relying on your own habitual way of managing conflict with jerks, you need to leverage a set of tried-and-true techniques. According to Thomas and Kilman's conflict management model, there are five common conflict management strategies: collaborate, compromise, avoid, accommodate, and compete.

When I work with organizations to remove workplace friction, I teach leaders and their employees how to leverage each of these conflict styles. Conflict situations may require use of any or a mix of these conflict styles. As such, they learn how to flex whichever of these styles are needed, depending on the conflict situation. Oftentimes, jerks tend to use the competing conflict style so that they can pursue their own interests and get what they want out of the situation at the expense of others. They don't value the relationship.

To create a jerk-free workplace, leaders must encourage the use of the collaborating style to achieve a win-win situation. When you use the collaborating style, both parties can get what they want. Both parties value the relationship and the outcome of the situation. This style takes work, but it is worth the investment for long-term satisfaction and successful relationships. For an effective collaboration to occur, each person must share their needs and objectives by being open and honest.

Note: If you would like to know how proficient your organization is in working with jerks and managing conflict, check out my conflict proficiency level chart by scanning the QR code below. I created this model to assess an organization's conflict proficiency.

SOLICIT FEEDBACK.

Leaders must solicit feedback not only from their leadership colleagues, but from their direct reports. This helps them keep their head on a swivel and do a pulse check to understand what's going on beneath the surface of the organization.

Asking for informal feedback during one-on-one conversations or during team meetings gives your team an opportunity to be open, honest, and vulnerable. Another way to solicit feedback is through anonymous surveys. This shows employees that you not only value their input, but that you are committed to making the necessary changes.

Note: If you are not soliciting informal feedback from your direct reports, this is how you can be perceived as a jerk! It shows that you don't care, you're dismissive, and you're not curious or engaged. When you encourage informal feedback, it gives employees an opportunity to be open, honest, and vulnerable.

COMMUNICATE WITH CLARITY.

Leaders need to improve their level of communication to provide clarity about what's expected and to set expectations. Oftentimes, environments are full of jerks due to poor communication. When there is a lack of clarity regarding what is expected, it cultivates an environment of confusion and chaos. It's costly, because it delays work from getting done and results in poor quality outputs. Employees get frustrated and upset when the goal is unclear. As such, leaders must set clear expectations and guidelines regarding what is expected by providing the rules of engagement and the background of the situation, as well as explaining the "why" so that employees don't feel kept in the dark about the course of action. They need a clear understanding about what action they are expected to perform.

ONE-ON-ONE CONVERSATIONS.

The most effective managers recognize that one-on-one conversations with their employees are not add-ons to their role—they are foundational to it. One-on-one conversations, when done the right way, help build stronger, more meaningful relationships between employees and their leaders. It builds trust, improves motivation, increases engagement, and boosts retention. Some leaders who use one-on-one conversations to only get status updates on projects and tasks are missing out on a golden opportunity to build a unique relationship with their employees. The meetings are one-sided and ineffective because they don't get to the heart of the situation. Instead, leaders should use the one-to-one conversations to ask emotionally charged questions that spark curiosity.

For example, during one-to-one conversations, ask questions like these:

"What's your win for the week?"

"What are you looking forward to the most when this project is complete?"

"What's got you frustrated the most about this situation?"

"What's draining your energy?"

"What's the source of your energy?"

When you ask these questions, not only will you learn about what employees are working on, you understand more about an employee, how they are feeling about the situation, and how you can support them. This is far more effective and meaningful than receiving status updates. Additionally, employees will be much more engaged and appreciate that you want to learn more about them.

Creating a jerk-free workplace takes courageous leadership. It can't be achieved overnight. It takes time. It takes a consistent

CREATING A JERK-FREE WORKPLACE THROUGH COURAGE

commitment from leaders to improve the culture. Not only must leaders stand up to jerks, but they must also hold themselves accountable if they are acting like jerks. This includes making a serious investment in developing social skills, leadership skills, and conflict management skills through training, coaching, and mentoring. A strong step in the right direction is for leaders to become curious about their teams and how they can support them. Start asking questions, solicit their feedback through one-on-ones or anonymous surveys. It takes time to create a jerk-free workplace. Don't get discouraged if you don't see significant progress overnight. Stay patient, resilient, and committed, and before you know it, you'll be on your way to creating a jerk-free workplace.

CHAPTER 8

Mind Games: Unraveling the Mystery of Emotional Shenanigans with Mustard and Bananas

Christina Reising

SPHR, SHRM-CP

Positivity Instigator & Innovation Igniter

linkedin.com/in/christinareising

orbitcoachingandconsulting.com

Christina, a holder of three certifications in emotional intelligence, is a powerhouse of transformation in the business world. Fueled by her passion for infusing emotional intelligence into the heart of every organization, she ignites the spark of change. With a dynamic array of projects and long-standing partnerships, Christina is your go-to guide for navigating the ever-evolving landscape of HR and people operations.

With two decades of experience, Christina has teamed up with over 200 companies, leading them through the maze of HR intricacies while fostering environments where teams flourish. Her mantra? People first, always. She is not just about policies and procedures but about championing individual well-being.

Christina is not your typical HR guru—she is a trailblazer. Whether she is pioneering a leadership academy in the fire service, contributing to the triumphant launch of a water park, or helping companies define their core values, Christina's impact knows no bounds.

And when it comes to those tough conversations, Christina knows the secret sauce. She helps family-owned businesses plan for the future, handles mass layoffs with empathy and grace, and navigates tricky situations with finesse.

Christina is not just a consultant; she is the driving energy that propels businesses forward.

• • •

"That's just weird," Avery remarked, her expression curious as she directed her gaze at Carly.

Carly paused, intrigued. "What's weird?"

"You peel your entire banana before eating it," Avery retorted.

This conversation unfolded during an emotional intelligence training I facilitated, and as you'll soon learn, it didn't end there.

"So what? Why does that make me weird? And where did that come from? I'm not even eating a banana right now. Besides, you eat mustard on everything. Hell, you walk around here with mustard packets in your pocket and eat the mustard right out of the packet at random times throughout the day," Carly countered, shocked.

"Yeah, that is weird," Maggie interjected, nodding in agreement. "I peel my banana from the top and continue to peel it as I eat it, but I don't eat mustard on everything."

"I peel my banana from the bottom, but I don't eat mustard on everything either," Dakota added.

"Okay, first off, I didn't say you were weird, Carly," Avery clarified. "Second, I don't eat mustard on my bananas, so I don't eat mustard on everything, but my banana needs to be green, or I won't eat it. Does that make me even weirder?"

Maggie smiled. "I think being weird is a good thing, but that's just how I was raised."

"I don't," Carly disagreed. "I'm different from most of my family, and I think that's a good thing, but they call me 'weird' and mean it as a bad thing. Can I just say, we've been talking about triggers, and 'weird' is a trigger word for me."

Dakota nodded empathetically. "Yeah, same here. It feels like judgment."

This training aimed to foster self-awareness and empathy and help participants excel as colleagues, leaders, and positive workplace role models. So, what's the mystery?

CONDIMENT CONFESSIONS AND FRUIT FIASCOS

Emotional intelligence (EI) refers to the ability to recognize, understand, and manage one's own emotions and those of others. It involves being aware of how emotions influence behavior and using that awareness to navigate social interactions and make decisions effectively.

On the other hand, emotional quotient (EQ) refers to a numerical measurement of a person's emotional intelligence. It's often measured through assessments. Hence, the objective of the training was to empower participants to enhance their EQ by fostering the development of their EI skills.

Emotional intelligence comprises four fundamental components essential for personal and professional success: self-awareness, self-management, social awareness, and relationship management.

- Self-awareness involves recognizing and understanding one's emotions, strengths, weaknesses, values, and motivations.
- Self-management entails constructively regulating emotions, impulses, and behaviors, including stress management, and maintaining a positive outlook.
- Social awareness involves empathizing with others' emotions, needs, and perspectives while being attentive to social cues.

- Relationship management focuses on building and maintaining healthy, positive relationships through effective communication, conflict resolution, and collaboration.

Together, these components form the foundation of emotional intelligence, enabling individuals to navigate social interactions, manage emotions effectively, and cultivate strong relationships in various aspects of life.

Now, let's revisit the scenario in the training room, where the topic of conversation unexpectedly shifted to mustard and bananas. How does this seemingly trivial discussion relate to the ability to recognize, understand, and effectively manage emotions individually and in relationships?

To find out, I decided to engage each person directly, asking them to articulate the emotions they were experiencing at the moment. Here's what they shared:

Avery let out a sigh. "I should've just kept quiet. All I wanted was a banana, and suddenly it made me think of Carly eating one yesterday at lunch. I honestly didn't mean anything by it."

"Yeah? Well, I feel like I'm under attack here," Carly replied defensively. "It's like I'm back at my childhood dinner table with my family, where every move I made was scrutinized. I'm a grown woman; I should be able to eat what I want without judgment."

"I'm feeling really overwhelmed right now," Maggie said, her voice trembling with anxiety. "Are we seriously arguing about food? Our job is already stressful enough."

Dakota shook her head in disbelief. "So, this is what they mean by self-management? I want to tell everyone to suck it up and move on so we can finish this training, but it's clear we need to address these emotions. Why are we even caught up in how or what someone eats? It's not like it's part of our job description."

Lightheartedly, I said, "So, I'm hearing that we all like bananas, but we have mixed emotions about mustard, right?"

Everyone chuckled, but I knew we were in a delicate place, so I asked, "Avery, do you know why you eat mustard on everything?"

Dakota was looking at me like, *Seriously? We're going to keep talking about mustard after I just said it isn't part of our job? Who is this lady, anyways?* But watch what happens next.

Avery shrugged. "I just like it."

I gently asked, "Do you know how long you've liked it?"

Avery pondered for a moment. "I don't know. I grew up eating mustard with my papa. It reminds me of him."

Curiosity piqued, I inquired, "Do you eat mustard specifically to remind yourself of him, or do you eat it to cover the taste of something you don't like? Or for some other reason?"

Avery's response was candid. "Both. I did that all the time growing up—to cover the taste of things. I still do it sometimes now, too. It's mainly a habit at this point, though. Plus, I'm eating more packets right now because I'm trying to quit smoking."

As Avery shared her memories of her grandfather and her struggle to quit smoking, the atmosphere in the room shifted, transforming into one of empathy and support. The conversation continued, weaving together personal stories, childhood memories, and heartfelt encouragement. Through this exchange, Avery's vulnerability became a catalyst for deeper connection and understanding within the group, nurturing a sense of camaraderie and mutual respect.

Ultimately, Avery apologized to Carly, clarifying her intent behind the seemingly insensitive remark. This acknowledgment, coupled with the group's shared experiences and empathetic responses, exemplified the power of emotional intelligence in fostering authentic connections and resolving conflicts.

COGNITIVE CAROUSEL

Though seemingly trivial, the discussion surrounding mustard and bananas unearthed a torrent of genuine and intense emotions for those involved. It's crucial to acknowledge that not everyone feels at ease sharing personal experiences, whether they revolve around childhood memories or struggles with quitting smoking, and that's perfectly acceptable.

This scenario poignantly reminds us how seemingly minor details can trigger emotional responses and profoundly affect interpersonal relationships. From my observations, such incidents are more prevalent in the workplace than is commonly acknowledged, influenced by factors ranging from individual personalities and cultures to organizational norms and what is deemed acceptable in the workplace.

In this specific case, the setting was conducive to open dialogue, which I facilitated. Yet, the outcomes of such conversations often remain unpredictable, with numerous potential trajectories. Unfortunately, many workplace conflicts of this nature culminate in damaged relationships, occasionally necessitating intervention from supervisors or human resources.

Emotions serve as invaluable data points, consciously and unconsciously shaping our behaviors.

Throughout my career, I've delved into countless investigations, testified, or served as an expert, handled a multitude of employee relations issues, addressed Equal Employment Opportunity Commission (EEOC) claims, and navigated unemployment cases. Across all these scenarios, a consistent theme emerged: emotions and the significance of our emotional responses. Emotions serve as invaluable data points, consciously and unconsciously shaping our behaviors. Recognizing and managing these emotions is crucial for fostering healthy workplace dynamics and effectively resolving conflicts.

The notion of "leaving emotions at the door" is a fallacy. Our brains aren't wired to compartmentalize emotions in such a manner. Understanding and managing our emotions is essential. Neuroscience illustrates that our brains meticulously process every experience and conversation we encounter.

It all begins at the base of our neck, where the spinal cord meets the brain. This marks the entry point for stimuli or inputs from the world around us. From there, they traverse to the limbic system, situated at the core of our brain—the emotional epicenter—where our feelings reside. Upon arrival, each stimulus promptly triggers an emotional response. We instinctively categorize events as either rewarding or threatening, good or bad.

Every stimulus we encounter triggers an emotional response before our rational mind engages.

For instance, receiving a promotion might elicit emotions of joy and accomplishment, while experiencing car trouble on the way to work could provoke anxiety or frustration. After traveling through the limbic system, stimuli journey to the frontal lobe, located behind our forehead, which is the hub of rational thinking and decision-making.

Every stimulus we encounter triggers an emotional response before our rational mind engages. Thus, we often feel before we think, occasionally leading to decisions influenced by emotion rather than logic. It's imperative to recognize that this process may differ for individuals contending with brain trauma or those with intellectual and developmental disabilities. Understanding this interplay between emotions and cognition is pivotal for navigating the intricacies of human experience.

Unlike personality traits and IQ, which exhibit relative stability over time, emotional intelligence is malleable and can be honed through practice. This is attributable to the brain's remarkable neuroplasticity—the capacity for change. By engaging in activities that foster emotional awareness, empathy, and self-regulation, individuals can fortify the neural pathways linked to emotional intelligence and increase their EQ.

Reinforcing connections between the limbic system (which is responsible for emotions) and the frontal lobe (which is responsible for rational thought) can help individuals enhance their adeptness at managing their emotions effectively.

ALMONDS, TWO! (NOT TOO.)

When a stimulus reaches the frontal lobe, it doesn't automatically turn us into great decision-makers. Emotions are our immediate reactions to what happens around us, quick and powerful, such as sudden bursts of fear or joy. While emotions tend to be intense and fleeting, feelings encompass more intricate and nuanced emotional states stemming from personal experiences, memories, and interpretations of events.

Upon asking Carly about her emotional state, her response wasn't singular. Rather, she expressed feeling personally attacked, a sentiment intertwined with underlying emotions such as anger, hurt, and distress. The sensation of being personally attacked typically triggers a potent emotional reaction, marked by feelings of vulnerability, defensiveness, or unease. In Carly's case, her body language—hunched posture, crossed arms, averted gaze—and her firm tone conveyed a palpable sense of vulnerability and defensiveness.

The brain houses two almond-shaped structures known as amygdalae, one in each hemisphere, nestled within the limbic system. Daniel Goleman, credited with introducing the concept of "amygdala hijack," highlights how these small yet powerful structures can occasionally take control of our rational thinking, dictating our emotional responses. Primarily tasked with processing emotions, especially those linked to survival instincts like fear or aggression, the amygdala plays a pivotal role in our fight-or-flight mechanism.

When faced with stimuli evoking strong emotions, the amygdala can swiftly trigger our body's fight-or-flight response, often before our rational mind fully comprehends the situation. Consequently, we may act impulsively, not paying any heed to the potential consequences. This is where the concept of "how can someone so smart do something so stupid" comes in—they're exhibiting a lack of emotional intelligence.

The effects of an amygdala hijack can be profound and immediate. When the amygdala takes over, it can feel as though intense emotions have temporarily overridden our rational thinking. This state of emotional overwhelm can persist until the amygdala's response subsides, which may take some time depending on the individual and the situation. During this period, it can be challenging to regain control and return to a state of calm and rationality. Understanding the dynamics of an amygdala hijack is crucial for developing strategies to manage our emotional reactions effectively and navigate challenging situations with greater clarity and composure. Thankfully, Carly was able to maintain her rational thinking even though she was having trouble managing her body language.

Earlier, Carly brought up the term "trigger," which resurfaces in the discussion on amygdala hijack. But what exactly constitutes a trigger? A trigger denotes any stimulus or event that elicits a profound emotional response or reaction from an individual. Triggers vary widely from person to person, encompassing an array of stimuli ranging from specific words to sounds, smells, images, situations, memories, or experiences. Frequently tied to past traumas or deeply entrenched emotional associations, encountering triggers can provoke heightened emotional reactions within a person. Given the multitude of stimuli encountered daily, recognizing and comprehending one's triggers is crucial for effectively managing emotions and navigating challenging circumstances.

UNLOCKING THE POWER OF EMOTIONAL INTELLIGENCE

Emotional intelligence is a cornerstone of personal and professional success, but how does it manifest in real life?

Self-aware individuals clearly understand their strengths, weaknesses, values, and aspirations. Starting with fundamental questions about identity, such as "Who am I?" and "What do I do?" and defining core values lays the foundation for better emotional management.

Proficient self-managers excel in regulating emotions, maintaining composure in challenging situations, and adapting to change. Strategies like monitoring internal dialogue and practicing positive self-talk can be pivotal in enhancing self-management skills.

Individuals with heightened social awareness can discern others' emotions and respond empathetically. This involves attentiveness to verbal and nonverbal cues and embracing diverse perspectives.

Effective relationship managers excel in communication, active listening, conflict resolution, and trust-building, which are essential for successful collaboration.

In the training session, empathy played a pivotal role in transforming the casual conversation about mustard and bananas into a profound exploration. Avery's vulnerability when sharing her memories sparked empathy within the group, promoting camaraderie and support by validating others' experiences and creating a safe space for dialogue.

THINK ABOUT HOW YOU THINK

Have you ever paused to consider how much of the stress you experience at work is due to the workplace itself, as opposed to your own perception of it? It's often not the physical environment that causes stress; rather, it's our interactions with colleagues or those in positions of authority, coupled with our interpretations of their behavior. It's not necessarily the tasks we perform, but our emotional responses to them. Take, for instance, two of my primary clients: firefighters and police officers. They frequently express their love for their jobs, despite their roles being widely acknowledged as being among the most stressful positions in our society.

Enhancing emotional intelligence involves recognizing that events usually don't impact us as much as our interpretation of those events, which are closely tied to our emotions. But why do we feel a certain emotion in response to an event? What other feelings accompany that initial emotion? Consider a scenario where Avery remarks to Carly that her way of eating a banana is weird. Carly interprets this as a personal attack because it triggers memories of hurtful treatment during family dinners, dinners she doesn't usually think about. While Avery didn't intend to attack Carly personally, Carly's interpretation of the comment led to hurt feelings.

In many cases, individuals tend to take things personally when, in reality, the situation isn't personal—at least, that's not how the other party (or parties) perceives it. What seems personal to one person might be entirely innocuous from the other party's perspective. While intentional and personal attacks certainly occur in the workplace, that's a topic deserving of its own discussion.

STRATEGIES FOR CULTIVATING A WORKPLACE THAT WORKS

In the dynamic landscape of modern workplaces, emotions often run as high as productivity goals. From the subtle nuances of office interactions to the complexities of team dynamics, navigating the emotional terrain of work can sometimes feel like solving a puzzle with unconventional pieces—as was the case with the discussion involving mustard and bananas. Yet, within this seemingly whimsical scenario, there lies a profound truth: Understanding and managing emotions is essential for cultivating a workplace that works. As we delve into strategies for individuals and employers, let us explore how cultivating a culture of emotional intelligence can lead to a workplace that functions and flourishes.

Individuals have a multitude of avenues through which they can enrich their emotional intelligence and interpersonal skills. One path involves improving self-awareness through practices like self-reflection, mindfulness meditation, or journaling, which aid in understanding emotions, identifying triggers, and recognizing biases. Cultivate curiosity and ask questions—not just of others but also of yourself. Explore what triggers your emotions, why you experience certain feelings and how you can navigate them effectively. Similarly, empathy can be honed through active listening, empathy-building workshops, and seeking out and embracing diverse viewpoints.

Effective communication, marked by clarity, respect, and attentiveness to nonverbal cues, lays the foundation for mutual understanding. Cultivating a mindset that embraces constructive feedback and acknowledges achievements nurtures a positive workplace atmosphere. Techniques such as stress management, work-life balance, and mindfulness of self and others further bolster emotional regulation.

Adopting habits like pausing before reacting, refraining from immediately jumping to conclusions, and practicing positive self-dialogue can enhance emotional intelligence. Seeking guidance from trusted confidants can offer invaluable insights for personal growth, culminating in a holistic approach to self-improvement that strengthens emotional intelligence and interpersonal bonds.

Employers wield significant influence over fostering their workforce's emotional intelligence and interpersonal adeptness. Initiatives such as facilitating opportunities for self-reflection, offering mindfulness training, and providing personal development resources can nurture self-awareness among employees. Empathy can be cultivated through workshops, employee resource groups, team-building exercises, and open communication channels.

Prioritizing clear and respectful communication, providing communication skills training, and emphasizing nonverbal communication's significance contribute to a positive organizational climate. Instituting frameworks for constructive feedback and recognition and supporting stress management and work-life balance aids in emotional regulation. Mentorship programs, coaching sessions, and leadership training offer tailored support for growing one's emotional intelligence. Integrating emotional intelligence metrics into performance evaluations underscores organizational commitment to these competencies. Additionally, offering counseling services, employee assistance programs, and wellness initiatives demonstrates an organization's dedication to employee well-being.

Fostering emotional intelligence is not solely the responsibility of employers within the workplace; it is a personal journey that individuals can embark on independently. Even in environments where employers do not prioritize emotional intelligence, individuals can take proactive steps to develop these skills for their own personal growth and well-being, by recognizing the importance of emotional intelligence and investing in self-awareness, empathy, and effective communication.

Mystery solved!

CHAPTER 9

Making Hybrid Work: Facilitating the Right Work from the Right Place at the Right Time

Wendy A. Cocke

Founder - Engineering Leadership Solutions

engineeringleadershipsolutions.com

makingflexwork.com

reimagineyourwork.com

Wendy Cocke, author of the bestselling books *Making Flex Work: Defining Success on Your Own Terms* and *Reimagine Your Work: Managing Your Career Like It's Your Business*, is the founder of Engineering Leadership Solutions, where she works with high-achieving, technical professionals and organizations who think about work differently.

A chemical engineer by training, she spent over twenty years leading technical teams in Fortune 500 companies prior to opening her own consulting company and joining the faculty at her alma mater, where she teaches engineering students "how work works." About ten years into her career, Wendy pursued a flexible work arrangement to find balance in all aspects of her life. She was told that it would stall her career, but little did they know that the change to her work schedule would be the catalyst that would propel her career to the next level.

As a working mother, Wendy has redefined success according to her values, balancing work and life so that she can drive results while still spending the quality time needed to raise her children and support her extended family. She believes that with her experience and her engineering mindset, she can help other people do the same.

> "This won't shock you at all, but I'm ten times more valuable to my company when I actually come to work and engage than when I'm at home."

Since publishing my first book, *Making Flex Work: Defining Success on Your Own Terms*, I've had hundreds of conversations about work effectiveness, so this wasn't entirely out of the ordinary, but this one caught me off guard.

As a two-time best-selling author and speaker focused on flexible work, people think I am advocating for everyone to be able to work from home, but, in reality, some work is more effective in one place versus the other, and some organizations are more effective in one style than the other. It's the balance between remote and in-person work that serves as the secret ingredient for the long-term success of flexibility. Together, throughout this chapter, we will evaluate your work and culture and how to make hybrid work for you.

What struck me with this specific text was that it came from a person who knows all of this, and yet, it wasn't until he had been going to the office for six months that he discovered the power of being in the office and sent me this text. Prior to that, he'd only been going to work because he was *supposed*—that is, told—to, but when he engaged in community and in-person discussions, he discovered why being in the office is important. Furthermore, he shared that he is now considering going into the office more than is required.

Simply telling people they need to go back to the office isn't enough.

I share this story with you as a word of caution. Simply telling people they need to go back to the office isn't enough—even sharing the "why" isn't enough; they need to feel it for themselves. So wherever you are on your hybrid work journey, while trying to find the right balance of in-person, hybrid, and virtual work options, know that it's critical to create opportunities for the team to feel the power of being together.

I hope you find value in the ideas that I share and that they will improve your odds of success. Simply put, they are about ensuring the right work from the right place at the right time.

THE RIGHT WORK

It's hard for many leaders to lose direct control of their teammates, which is what is necessary to provide them with flexibility. As long as the company is getting exactly what it needs to be successful, and the teammate is getting exactly what they need to feel balanced and energized, then there are infinite ways to get work done. Creatively managing these options sets excellent leaders apart from average ones. More importantly, as we are shifting into a hybrid workforce, teammates are going to be looking for leaders who have embraced this sort of creativity.

I encourage you to embrace new ideas and look for ways to incorporate them into your framework. There is no right or wrong way to achieve success; it's a journey. Generally speaking, there are two types of arrangements: "traditional," aka 9-5, the thing most people did prior to 2020, and "nontraditional," with the most common being flexible (taking a fluid approach to how and where the work is done), hybrid (mixing remote and in-person work) and remote (not having an on-site presence).

Regardless of the arrangement, good leadership is about facilitating work in a way that best meets the needs of the company and the team. As a leader, you should set clear expectations for performance and, if you provide flexibility, it's even more critical to have these expectations clearly outlined. As a refresher on objective setting, follow the process described by Doran, Miller, and Cunningham in 1981 and make them SMART.

- Specific: What do you want the person to deliver?
- Measurable: How will you know if the product they deliver is good?
- Achievable: Is this something they are capable of doing within the agreed-upon arrangement?
- Relevant: What does the business need and how can those needs be met?
- Time-bound: When would you like this task or project to be done? Is there any benefit to them being done sooner? How do they fit in the overall priority ranking?

ESTABLISH ROUTINE CHECK-INS

Teammates need to understand the flexible arrangement will only last as long as it's working for everyone, so establishing how and when you will determine whether everything is on track is important. Some questions to consider:

- Is success based on the delivery of a work product?
- What could impact the continuation of the arrangement?
- What timeframe would each side need to change the arrangement?

COMMUNICATE YOUR NONNEGOTIABLES

Teammates need to know how their role impacts the business and what options are available to them. It's also important that you communicate changes and exceptions early so teammates can prepare and respond accordingly. The best practice is at least a two-week notice. Think through each role on your team. Are there roles that require in-person interactions with customers, equipment, or sensitive information? They may need to be present more often. Is the team already scattered across the country or globe? Are there roles that need to accommodate multiple time zones? Are there jobs that are primarily individual work? These roles may allow for more flexibility. Other things to consider and communicate include:

- Which times and occasions do you need everyone to be in-person?
- What are your communication expectations for remote work?
- Who pays for travel to the office when needed?

BUILD COMMUNITY

Today more than ever, people are leveraging flexible work arrangements. You might only see some teammates once or twice a year, while you may never meet others in person at all. People naturally chit-chat before an in-person meeting but sit quietly typing before a virtual one. Leverage the dead space during the first few minutes of a virtual meeting to intentionally build connections to make your working time more productive. Examples include:

- Ask open-ended questions.
- Use free online brain teasers.
- Share resources, training insights, and other career development information.

THE RIGHT PLACE

When I started working (at the "turn of the century," as my teenage son calls it), phones were exclusively used for talking and computers had to be attached to the wall to access the internet. Today, we have a variety of options for getting work done effectively. As fast as things have evolved in the last twenty years, that change will only accelerate in the future. By allowing yourself to hear your employees' struggles and encouraging them to bring creative solutions to you, you can shape the work in countless ways.

Does your teammate have a device, gadget, application, set-up, or anything else that will make them more effective? To be a supportive leader, it's imperative that you see all options as possibilities and attempt to envision a way to make them work, as opposed to identifying reasons why they won't.

If you are serious about supporting hybrid work, there is more work for you than just saying *yes*. When you begin to give some people (or everyone) the ability to flex in and out of the office, it can affect the way your space is utilized, the technology needed for the job, and how people interact—including the potential for jealousy. As the leader, you have a lot to consider, but if you have the time and energy to do it right, you can position yourself as the person, department, or company that everyone will want to work for.

ASSESS YOUR SPACE

Traditional office spaces were not designed for hybrid work. Most are either filled with doors and large private spaces that will be underutilized in a hybrid environment, or have open floor plans originally intended to increase collaboration, but which have very little privacy and can be distracting in the virtual world as a result.

Here are some things to consider:

- How is space currently divided and utilized? Does that strategy drive the business forward?
- How will you minimize the visual distraction of the rest of the office environment and the background noise?
- Do you have enough conference room space and technology to support the video calls? What AV upgrades does your facility need?

EVALUATE YOUR EQUIPMENT NEEDS

Many people express specific workstation requirements to be effective at their job, and while some are legitimate, others are likely just a preference. As a leader, proactively thinking about how you will make sure that everyone can work successfully is critical to the success of hybrid work.

- Will people have assigned seats or will there be a sharing strategy, including who shares with whom and where personal supplies are stored?
- What equipment will be on-site, and what will travel back and forth with individual teammates?
- What specialized equipment will need to be duplicated for office and remote locations? Who pays for it?

HELP TEAMMATES FIND VALUE IN THE OFFICE

When people understand the reason for coming to the office, they not only do it willingly, they also move the business forward. Collaborative, creative, and strategic work is often more effective when we work in the same physical space. The opposite can be true for heads-down, focused work, due to the potential for distractions.

Here are some examples of work to consider be completed in-person:

- Celebrating a milestone or accomplishment.
- Training and onboarding new teammates.
- Working through information where details are important.
- Needing a big block of time (three to four hours) to accomplish the task.
- Workshops that require breakout group time.

THE RIGHT TIME

When everyone is together physically, it's easy to see work happen, but it's also easy to mistake presence for productivity. As a leader, when your team isn't within eyesight, you must trust that you have assigned the right amount of work to everyone, and accept that when high quality work is delivered, it doesn't matter when and where it happened.

With today's technology, work can happen anywhere. Whether it's a teleconference by the pool, a video call from a parking lot, or a group huddled together in a conference room, work is work. Understanding this is what sets excellent leaders apart from the average ones.

Once you let go of the idea that successful employees must be able to come to the office on a regular basis, you won't be limited to job candidates living in your area. Additionally, as traditional work constructs continue to be broken down, top talent will no longer be limited to jobs in their geographical location and will be able to choose not only what role they take, but who they want to work for. This means that being the best leader around isn't going to be good enough. You need to get proficient at understanding what you need done and setting clear expectations the first time, creating an environment where teammates are honest about their workload and are motivated to ask for more, establishing regular check-ins to ensure ongoing alignment through answering questions, not asking them, and being comfortable with a final product that isn't *exactly* what you envisioned as long as it meets your needs.

EXPECT TO BE INCLUSIVE OF REMOTE TEAMMATES

If there is another human in your space, you look at them when you talk. This means a virtual teammate can quickly be cut out of a discussion (even in a conference call with video capability) unless everyone is focused on not letting that happen. Here are some things to consider:

- How will you make sure the remote teammate is included in "offline" decisions, like informal hallway or drop-by discussions?
- What topics will be discussed in a totally virtual environment, which require face-to-face meetings, and which can be conducted hybridly?
- What types of meetings will require the team's cameras to be on and which can be off-camera?

EXPECT TO SEE EACH OTHER

Virtual meetings have fundamentally changed how business can be done by breaking physical distance assumptions and bringing people together who would have otherwise never seen each other, but they are amplifying our bad behaviors. Gone are the days of sitting in a meeting, watching people check their phones or type away on their laptops instead of paying attention: now they simply refuse to turn on their camera. Behind us are the days when someone might step out of a meeting to answer a call; now they just mute their line and start a second conversation. Then there's the worst offender of all: "Can we record this?" They might as well just say, "I'm not going to pay attention but want to be able to replay later just in case someone says something I need to refer to." As a leader, you establish the rules of engagement, and I encourage you to set the expectation and example that video will be used as much as possible. The biggest pushback I get to video use is the excuse about not being camera-ready. Here are a few easy tips to overcome that obstacle:

- A virtual background can make a messy room disappear.
- A jacket or cardigan can transform a tank top into an outfit.
- A scarf or pullover can hide your t-shirt.
- Jewelry or makeup can make you look put-together.

By turning cameras on, teams build closer relationships because it's easier to bond with people we see. Video allows you to make a more lasting impression with the other attendees in the meeting because you aren't a disembodied voice or a motionless icon. You show the others you respect them when you are present and engaged. By turning your camera on, you have an accountability partner—other people's eyeballs—to help you make good choices with your time. Like many people, I love being efficient and I also love to multitask. That's the problem with the on camera meetings; they prevent us from doing two things at once. People like to pretend that they aren't distracted, but how much more effective would our virtual meetings be if we were all fully present?

- What if we knew what was being asked of us in the context of the discussion when our name was called?
- What if we could absorb the entire meeting and identify inconsistencies with or "watch outs" in what was being presented so that we could be more efficient as a collective?
- What if we were all actively taking notes so that the next time the topic came up we all were prepared to pick right up where we left off?
- Wouldn't we be much more productive overall?

EXPECT EMPLOYEES TO BUILD FLEXIBILITY INTO THEIR PERSONAL LIFE TOO

Flexibility is a two-way street. For any of this to work, it's crucial that teammates have their personal lives set up in such a way that it never gets in the way of an unexpected work request. Just like they should have back-up plans at work in case they have to be out of the office, they should plan ahead to have the same provisions and setup at home. There should be no reason that, given sufficient notice, they are unable to meet any work request. This may mean securing child or elder care even for times they aren't planning to come to the office. Remember, it's only going to be successful in the long run because it's flexible. Success in a long-term flexible work arrangement necessitates that the company gets what it needs to deliver results.

FINAL THOUGHTS

For most of the history of corporate work, the idea that someone could be successful doing things differently than their peers was rarely talked about. People on nontraditional schedules—mostly moms—hid in the shadows, hoping those around them wouldn't know about the secret arrangement they had secured. It was as if they feared the scarlet letter that would be placed on them, and I was one of them. I had worked a nontraditional schedule for years in secret before I was challenged by a bold HR leader to become more than just a technical leader: to be an authentic leader in the fullest sense of the word. A leader who provided an example of a different way to be successful.

As a leader, if you have the political capital and the safety net to do so, I encourage you to take a risk and not hide how you make it all work. Let those around you see your struggle, let them see your reality. Only you know your reality, but by letting others see what you are balancing, you, too, can help change the future for those who follow and those looking for an example. More importantly, once you fully embrace flexible work, you will be the one that other leaders look to understand the "new norm," what is acceptable, and what they can expect from those who come next.

As a people-leader myself, I've learned quite a few things. When it comes to leading people, you have a choice. You can either force your team to conform to your needs, or you can adjust your needs to accommodate each individual. There is no right or wrong way to lead teams, but if you, as the leader, are willing to customize your approach to meet each teammate where they are, people will flock to you. The ability to make everyone feel like they are heard, valued, and important to the overall mission can position you as the leader for whom everyone wants to work.

You can either force your team to conform to your needs, or you can adjust your needs to accommodate each individual.

Now more than ever, it's likely that one or more of your employees will be asking for flexibility. Maybe you will make the decision to provide flexibility for child or elder care needs. Maybe you will provide flexibility out of the desire to support physical and mental health. Maybe you will make the decision to leverage flexibility as the most important retention tool in your managerial toolbox. As long as you can ensure that the work is getting done, I challenge you to start *Making Hybrid Work* today.

Chapter 10

Be a Builder in Everything You Do Every Day

Doug Reitz

Dad, Husband, Builder, Speaker, Owner of MWC

linkedin.com/in/doug-reitz

Dougreitz.blog

Recognized as a highly respected builder in California, Doug's influence extends beyond building projects. He has also been instrumental in shaping the industry by speaking at events and facilitating workshops across the state that delve into the creation of effective teams, leadership, sustainable company cultures, and industry best practices. Also, his commitment to education has spanned over twenty years of teaching classes on leadership, ethics, and advanced construction techniques at California State University, Fresno.

In construction, Doug has had a remarkable journey, constructing projects totaling over one billion dollars. His adventure began at Fresno State, where he graduated with a degree in Construction Management in 1991. A passion was ignited in Doug, not just for construction, but for leadership, mentorship, and building those around him.

Doug's new book, *BUILD: A Blueprint for Constructing Success in Leadership and Life*, will be published in the fall of 2024.

The tools in *BUILD* are the same tools Doug and his core team use to shape the culture and standards at his company. They have seen a remarkable fourfold increase in volume over a decade. This growth, managed with precision and care, ensures that the company's standards and culture not only endure but continue to thrive.

Building is one of the most powerful tools anyone can have in their toolbox.

"Building is a tool?" you might ask. "I thought you needed *tools* to build buildings!"

Yes, building is a *tool*!

Building allows you to take an incremental approach to building solutions, trust, relationships, and consensus, much like you would build a building. You start with a good foundation, then a structure, infrastructure, and the finishing touches. It takes time to build a building that will stand the test of time, as it does when you build solutions, relationships, consensus, and trust.

How do I know? Well, there came a point in my career where I was so focused on success and what everyone else was doing wrong that I nearly lost my wife, my friends, and my job, all at the same time. Everything came crashing down. I learned some valuable lessons during some exceedingly difficult times, which I detailed in my book *BUILD: A Blueprint for Constructing Success in Leadership and Life*.

This chapter will introduce you to the blueprint for becoming a builder and how to use it as a tool in leadership, showing you the importance of checking your ego, guiding you through everyday conflicts and challenges, and offering a framework that not only resolves immediate issues but paves the way for enduring success.

Be a *builder* in everything you do, every day, and that is *When Work Works*!

SECTION 1 — WHEN WORK DOESN'T WORK

It was just after lunch when Tim called and wanted to see me in the home office. His normally calm demeanor was not present this time. The fifteen-minute drive seemed like an hour.

Tim Marsh was my supervisor, mentor, and second dad. We worked together side by side for twenty-four years. Over the years, we both grew. He took over as president of the company and I moved up to be this particular venture's Project Executive.

I had a feeling the call had something to do with the fact I had been butting heads with the architect and inspector for the last couple of weeks. The inspection team did not understand the pressure that a $130 million project brings to the project executive. This was the largest single school project ever constructed in the state of California and it all rested on my shoulders.

As I walked into Tim's office, he had an uncharacteristically firm look on his face as he asked me to sit down. I said, "Man, Tim, what's up?"

"Well," Tim said, "I just got a call from the inspector, and he has requested that you be removed from the project."

"He can't do that!" I yelled. "He is the one with the issue and I am busting my ass to get the work done. I am not the problem, he is!"

Tim sat in silence for what seemed like an eternity, then said, "Doug, I know you see the challenges and where the project needs to go. You are right."

"Thank you," I said.

"But, sometimes being right and driving so hard is not the best approach," he continued. "Do you really think the architect and the inspector are trying to make the project fail?"

"It sure seems like it," I said.

BE A BUILDER IN EVERYTHING YOU DO EVERY DAY

He looked at me with a startled look.

"Okay, no, I do not think they are doing it on purpose," I clarified. "They have always tried to do the right thing and keep the project moving... so why aren't they doing it now? This is too important to me."

"To you?" Tim asked.

"Yes, my career is riding on this. You put me in charge, and I have to lead the charge up the hill, just like you have always taught me. I want my family to be proud. I want you to be proud. I want my team to be proud."

He said, "Doug, that is a lot of 'I's. So, *you* charged the hill, huh?"

"Yes, every single day!"

Tim continued, "Turn around and look down that hill and tell me what you see."

I said, "What do you mean? The hill is just a figure of speech."

"Yes, it is, but it is real," he said. "From where I am sitting, you are charging the hill stronger and faster than anyone, and that is the problem. But when I look down the hill, I see the inspector, the architect, the owner, and your team still standing at the bottom. Doug, they are not following you up the hill. Your ideas are great, you can see it, but you are not building confidence and trust in your team, so they do not want to follow you."

It is not about you.
It is all about the team.

That statement hit me like a ton of bricks.

I loved my team. But my drive to make it happen was holding everything back.

"Doug, it is not about you. It is all about the team. That is what you need to focus on. You have to think, what would a builder do?"

"What do you mean, a builder? I am in the office. I am not a carpenter."

"No Doug, not a carpenter. A *builder*. But they are remarkably similar. A carpenter takes raw materials, reads the plans, and assembles the materials into something that serves a new purpose. I need you to do that with your team. Build consensus, build trust, and build relationships. You are not doing that right now, and that is what you need to do: be a *builder*," Tim explained.

I said, "Okay, Tim, I will do my best."

As the saying goes, it is always darkest before dawn. Over the next few months, instead of things getting better, they started to spiral. Little did I know, the incident with the inspector was just the beginning. My family, friends, and coworkers were all disappointed in me.

Looking back now, I had only wanted what was best for my team. But, in my mind, I did not need anyone to help. I was wrong. Instead of building trust and long-lasting relationships, my actions did exactly the opposite. My team didn't trust me and didn't believe I had their best interests in mind.

It was the lowest point in my life, and I had to make a change.

SECTION 2 — THE PHILOSOPHY

BUILDING WILL BRIDGE THE GAP

In my situation, I had some major things to change, and I knew it would take a long time. However, I also had great people supporting me. So, I made the choice to tear down the things that were not working and to build a new way of addressing problems and leading my team. Going through the process took years. I finally realized anything can be solved by being a builder.

I started by listening to the people around me and taking what they said to heart. Then I put a plan together that consisted of what I had to change and do differently. Finally, I took the step into uncertainty and put my plan into action, starting to build those around me.

Take a look at things in your life and put fear and ego to the side for a moment. What can you change that would make things more effective for your team?

Like me, you may be frustrated with the team's lack of communication, trust, information, direction, or understanding of the goal. Maybe it's a lack of drive, skill, or motivation in the people around you. Or, as it was for me, it may be *you* that is causing the problem.

Whether you are in a leadership role or you are a part of someone's staff, it is your responsibility to solve the problem with your team. You need to check your ego and listen to learn. In every challenge, when there is a gap that needs to be spanned to move forward effectively as a team, ask yourself one question: What do we need to build?

> *I started by listening to the people around me and taking what they said to heart. Then I put a plan together that consisted of what I had to change and do differently. Finally, I took the step into uncertainty and put my plan into action, starting to build those around me.*

Picture yourself on the shore of a river and the thing you would like to do or have on the other side. It seems impossible to reach your goal. Standing there, you know where you are and can see where you want to be, but the river is the thing that stops you. You must build a bridge to get across. It is the same thing with your team at work. If you are in conflict, you need to build a bridge of consensus, to improve a relationship, you need to build a bridge of trust, and if they need a new skill, you need to build a bridge of shared knowledge and technique.

BUILDING WILL BRING SUCCESS

As a leader, your duty is to take a step back from any challenging situation to be able to see both sides of it and, then, lead your team with purpose, finding the best solution. By realizing you don't know what you don't know, you implement a mindset of listening to learn both sides. When your team sees you listening to all sides, they will want to come to the table to help solve the challenge together. However, before you can use them, your team must believe you have *their* best interests at heart, as well as the best interests of the team. It takes time to build trust, respect, and faith in you and your team, but it is well worth the effort. The following are the benefits of being a builder:

- Being a builder will help you counteract the desire to get a quick fix or reward.
- Being a builder will help you bring people out of their corners and to the table to discuss issues.
- Being a builder is a long-term process, where you support the people around you until they can fly on their own.
- Being a builder is about doing things differently in the future, so that you are more effective and efficient than you were in the past.
- Being a builder will make you a stronger leader as you lead through the challenges you face every day.

Remember, in every learning experience, challenge, or failure, there is a gap—something that needs to be done, implemented, or accomplished. Something needs to be built to span the gap, and you are the one to build it.

SECTION 3 – THE PROCESS

LISTEN. PLAN. BUILD. – A BLUEPRINT TO HELP YOU LEAD AND SOLVE CHALLENGES.

"Listen. Plan. Build." is the methodical process for addressing a challenge. It allows you to gather information, plan, take action, and adapt, over and over, until you reach your goal. Here is the foundation of what each step entails.

Listen
Gather information without bias.

Plan
Create tasks or designate research that needs to be done to formulate a plan.

Build
Take action!

Your job as a leader and problem solver is to listen to those around you, put a plan together with your team, and then execute that plan. As you approach a challenging issue, remember, emotions may be running high, and motives may differ. It is human nature to be emotional in challenging situations because of personal investment, reputation, or even money that could be lost if something goes wrong. Your job is to recognize it and tactically let it play out in a controlled manner.

"Listen. Plan. Build." is the process that makes your team or mentees:

1. Feel they have been heard.
2. Feel they have contributed to the plan.
3. Take ownership of and action in the solution.

As you go through the process, write down all of the information you gathered. Here's an example.

LISTEN

To listen means "to gather information." It could be written, or verbal. You will be put into difficult situations where you don't agree with the person you are talking to. They may even be attacking you and your knowledge. This is the most important time to listen.

Your mindset should be that of a detective. You must detach from the emotion and learn all you can. You may learn that your perspective is skewed or completely wrong as a result of limited information.

When approaching a problem, think to yourself: I could be wrong; there may be information I am missing, and it is causing a misunderstanding; or the other person is wrong and I need to understand what is driving their thought process. In any of these cases, you must engage in active listening to gain a greater perspective.

Let's look at an example: my issue from the story above.

I gathered the team, and we had a very direct conversation about the things I needed to improve upon. This was very difficult, because the problem being solved was me.

Here are a few things my team came up with:

LISTEN

1. Too driven
2. Doesn't listen
3. Always had the best idea
4. Not a team player

It was very awkward, but they were letting me know what I needed to do better. Once we had my list, we needed to put a strategic plan together to get more effective results.

PLAN

For each of the items listed under "LISTEN," we drew an arrow to the right to the "PLAN" column and started working on a plan to address each of the items listed under "LISTEN."

Any plan must focus on the overall mission or what is best for the goal. In this case, changing how I approached problems, solutions, and my team when trying to achieve a goal were the desired outcomes. Here is what we came up with:

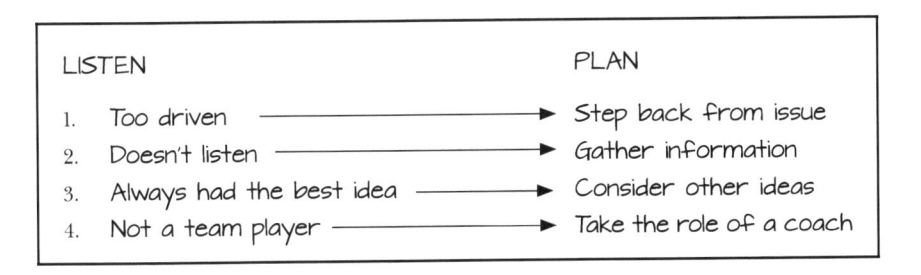

LISTEN	PLAN
1. Too driven	Step back from issue
2. Doesn't listen	Gather information
3. Always had the best idea	Consider other ideas
4. Not a team player	Take the role of a coach

A good plan serves two purposes. The first is that it gives you something to target or shoot for when you are dealing with the heavy details and tasks. Secondly, it gives you a measuring stick to see how you are progressing. Remember, it is an iterative process. You must approach it in increments. Since my team was involved, they could also hold me accountable if I strayed from the plan.

As a builder, I want you to know that the plan you and your team come up with is a tool to achieve the end goal of what you are trying to build. There will be successes and setbacks. You must adapt, reorient your plan, and always keep building.

BUILD

When you get to the "BUILD" phase, you could experience a feeling of hesitation. Even though you have done your best to vet all the possibilities, there is still uncertainty as to what could happen, and you may possibly find out something you didn't expect. Avoid experiencing analysis paralysis; there is no perfect plan.

The actions we would take to implement the plan are noted in the "BUILD" column:

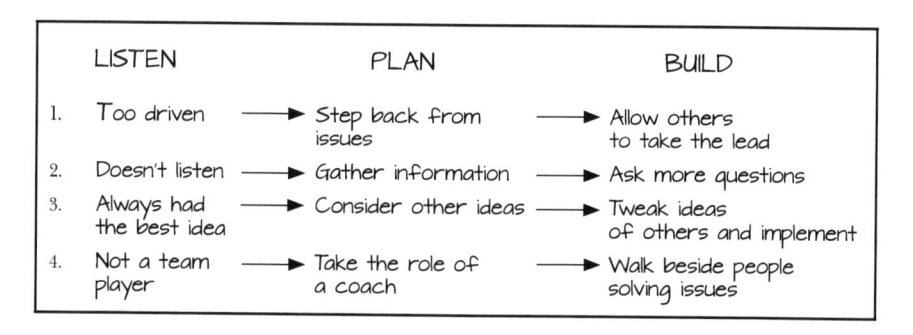

	LISTEN	PLAN	BUILD
1.	Too driven	→ Step back from issues	→ Allow others to take the lead
2.	Doesn't listen	→ Gather information	→ Ask more questions
3.	Always had the best idea	→ Consider other ideas	→ Tweak ideas of others and implement
4.	Not a team player	→ Take the role of a coach	→ Walk beside people solving issues

"BUILD" is the hardest step in the process, because you must take a step into uncertainty. It is when all the flaws in your plan will become strikingly evident or your plan will be confirmed to be correct or incorrect. The second hardest aspect of the process? To realize there were flaws in your plan and that you need to make corrections. Pushing through a "proven bad idea" because of ego can be detrimental to you, your team, and the project.

The "Listen. Plan. Build." tool must be used as a loop. As you take action, continue listening and planning repeatedly as new information comes to light. You will not be able to entirely avoid setbacks and failures, but because you are moving forward incrementally, the failures and setbacks will be smaller and easier to overcome. That will lead to a smoother path to success.

SECTION 4 — BUILD FOR A CAUSE BIGGER THAN YOURSELF

I am still a very driven person, but being a builder has changed my mindset so that I now approach challenges in a different way. It slows me down and allows me to see a bigger picture. Yes, I still slip, and my team calls me out, but that is part of the process. Mahatma Gandhi once said, "The best way to find yourself is to lose yourself in the services of others." Serving, or *building*, others is the essence of what Gandhi was saying. You will learn more about yourself by *building* others.

For me, it is all about being a builder in everything I do every day. I know I will never achieve perfection; the bar is high. However, it gives me something to aspire to when challenges arise. It is a cause bigger than me.

Building is not just for the construction industry; you can be a builder in your own field and in your community. Insurance carriers build stability, accountants build financial security, bus drivers build connections for their community, sanitation workers build clean cities. Everyone can be a builder for a cause bigger than themselves.

Fred Rogers said, "If you could only sense how important you are to the lives of those you meet; how important you can be to the people you may never even dream of. There is something you leave at every meeting with another person."

You will pass on knowledge that the team can use to solve a problem in the future when you are not there.

You will pass on knowledge that the team can use to solve a problem in the future when you are not there.

You may be thinking that you have tried to build others, but they just don't get it, or they don't acknowledge it. I am here to tell you that it is working. You just may not be seeing it, yet. Building is not a short-term game; it is the effect you have over time.

All great leaders are builders. So, when you are facing a gap, get stuck or frustrated, or find yourself facing a challenge that seems insurmountable, take a breath and ask yourself, *What do I need to build?* The answer will put you on a path to be an amazing leader, and that is truly "*When Work Works.*"

CHAPTER 11

Crafting Intentional Interactions at Work: In-Person Gatherings to Solve Business Problems and Cultivate Workplace Culture

Jeff Nally

PCC, SHRM-SCP

Chief Coaching Officer, Chief Human Resources Officer, Executive Coach & Professional Speaker

nallygroup.com/whenworkworks

nallygroup.com

linkedin.com/in/jeffnally

https://coachsource.com/

Jeff creates intentional interactions in the workplace so everyone can be better humans at work. He helps companies apply brain-based solutions and the science of human interaction in the workplace to increase engagement, accountability, and performance. He is a frequent keynote speaker at leadership, workplace culture, and human resource conferences, including the Society for Human Resource Management (SHRM) national and state conferences.

More than thirty years of corporate experience, coaching more than 400 executives, and crafting leadership solutions at Fortune 100 companies enable Jeff to bring proven approaches to help leaders and teams in any size organization. Jeff is the Chief Coaching Officer and Chief HR Officer at CoachSource, the world's most experienced coaching company. He is president of Nally Group Inc., focused on the science of leadership and intentional interaction in the workplace. Jeff is co-author of *Rethinking Human Resources and Humans@Work*.

He is past chair of the Kentucky SHRM State Council, past president of Louisville SHRM, and a former board member of the SHRM Foundation. Jeff was named one of the "Twenty People to Know in Human Resources" by Business First of Louisville and was the 2021 recipient of the Thomas J. Leonard Coach Humanitarian Award.

• • •

I was on a flight when I saw the news flash on my phone: "Humana To Vacate Iconic Headquarters Building in Downtown Louisville."

My heart sank as fond memories of the ten years I spent working in that landmark building rushed back to me. It was more than just a building to me. It was an intentional space that sparked employee engagement, lifelong friends, and so much more.

Ironically, I was flying to California to lead the first in-person, all-team gathering at CoachSource, a global provider of executive coaches to companies. Our company has been virtual since its inception seventeen years ago, and I pondered what intentional interactions in the workplace, workspaces, and in-person interactions mean for humans at work—and what they don't mean.

If you're a leader, human resources professional, or event planner, you're probably struggling with maintaining a good balance of virtual, in-person, and hybrid interactions. Perhaps you're grappling to find the balance between self-directed work, team collaboration, project teams, or committees attempting to accelerate their results and performance. When I speak at conferences and corporate workshops to help clients apply the science of human interaction in the workplace, I see their frustrations melt away when they learn how to craft intentional interactions and gatherings.

In this chapter, I'm sharing my own experiences, drawing examples from two companies—one where I worked several years ago, and one where I currently lead HR and executive coaching. At both companies, I created intentional interactions and gatherings to solve business problems, deepen engagement, and improve relationships at work. I'm also sharing best practices for crafting intentional interactions in your workplace and during gatherings.

HOW YOUR WORKPLACE AND GATHERING SPACE CAN SPARK EMPLOYEE ENGAGEMENT—AND MORE

Like many residents of Louisville, Kentucky, I was a teenager when Humana announced an architectural design competition for their new headquarters, the subsequent award of the Michael Graves design, and eventual construction of the Humana Building. I watched all this unfold with fascination.

From 1983 to 1985, it was a focal point of community intrigue and launched a revitalization of downtown Louisville, which had declined through the 1970s and early 1980s, but its design and construction were not without controversy. It's a quirky building that looks somewhat like a twenty-seven-story cash register. It was constructed with contrasting materials, including granite, marble, glass, and bronze. The building was ahead of its time and seemed out of place among a skyline of glass and steel high-rises. Nevertheless, I aspired to work in that building someday, and, for almost a decade, I would lead the executive coaching practice at Humana.

CREATING AN INTENTIONALLY WARM WELCOME ON DAY ONE

My favorite design element was the Main Street entrance. On my very first day at Humana, I entered into a low-ceilinged area, went through two sets of heavy bronze doors, and then stepped into the expansive lobby, with marble walls of various colors soaring several stories high, interior balconies, and "windows" that opened onto a neo-classical atrium.

For me, though, what was most stunning about stepping into that space was seeing one of my new coworkers standing in the center of that gorgeous lobby, waiting to welcome me. They shook my hand, told me about the building, and let me catch my breath from the adrenaline rush of starting a new job. They took me on a tour of the key spaces where I would meet with colleagues, collaborate with my team, and perform my work.

That moment of inspiration on "Day One" became a tradition I volunteered to recreate every time we added a new member to our team. There really was nothing like having a human being *and* the Humana Building warmly welcoming you on the first day of your new job. Meeting your new employee at the front door creates a memorable experience and personable start to their job.

INTENTIONAL INTERVIEW SPACES PUT CANDIDATES AT EASE

Over time, there were other spaces in the Humana Building where I created intentional interactions. I loved interviewing candidates on the south side of the twenty-fifth floor, which overlooked downtown Louisville and had floor-to-ceiling bay windows that were almost two stories tall. It was a quiet space for interviews, with comfortable chairs. The inspiring sunlit view wrapped around our conversation and made the space feel more like a fireside chat with a friend than an interview in a stark office. The setting put candidates at ease and signaled that I was intentionally creating a safe space for them to be their best selves during a traditionally stressful conversation.

WHEN WORKSPACES DEEPEN EMPLOYEE ENGAGEMENT

The Humana Building was an integral part of my day-to-day work that deepened my engagement: training leaders with state-of-the-art learning facilities; coaching executives in quiet, secluded spaces; lunch from restaurant-quality food stations in the cafeteria; working out in the underground gym; and meetings with colleagues in a variety of conference and meeting rooms. These were all happy times in a stunning workplace that drew me closer to the organization.

Over the years, Humana intentionally redesigned spaces so employees could collaborate easily and hold large gatherings. At every turn, they bathed the interior with vibrant colors, natural light, and art to inspire the senses—all of which contribute to deeper employee engagement.

It's not a perfect building. There were significant investments in repairs and maintenance. Times change, the workplace needs change, hybrid and virtual work arrangements require less office space, and nothing lasts forever. Not even a grand gem like the Humana Building.

BUILDINGS DO NOT CREATE MEANING

A building is not its people. Materials do not create meaning. A workspace is only as vibrant as the intentional interactions between the people inside living out their dreams, their talents, energies, and wisdom creating something larger than themselves.

The Humana Building taught me to never underestimate the power that intentional spaces have to attract and recruit talent, engage employees, inspire clients and collaborators, foster friendships, and generate "pride of place" in the work that we do. Your workplace does not need to be a gleaming corporate tower to create intentional interactions and impact.

> *A workspace is only as vibrant as the intentional interactions between the people inside living out their dreams, their talents, energies, and wisdom creating something larger than themselves.*

I'm now Chief HR Officer and Chief Coaching Officer at CoachSource, an all-virtual company. We've never had an office, and our team is scattered around the globe. Reflecting on the value of inspiring workspaces like the Humana Building may seem old-fashioned as hybrid and all-virtual workplaces like CoachSource become more pervasive. And yet, our human needs—and the business needs—for community, collaboration, and relationships are greater than ever. The value we create in person is enhanced and accelerated when we convene at inspiring workspaces, whether it's the Humana building, a hotel meeting space, or a modest retreat center.

If you're leading people in all-virtual or hybrid workplaces, be even more intentional about creating in-person interactions so participants know the purpose for gathering and the expected outcomes.

WHEN AN ALL-VIRTUAL COMPANY HAS ITS FIRST INTENTIONAL IN-PERSON GATHERING

It's a typical, yet not so typical story: a start-up company begins in the living room of our founder and CEO, Brian Underhill, and grows into CoachSource, a global professional services firm. The not so typical part is that, after seventeen years in operation, with over a thousand people in the organization, we've never had an office. Sounds great, but something was missing.

A new approach to the client experience led to adding twelve roles, creating account teams, expanding the C-suite, and shifting from part-time, contract positions to full-time, internal positions— all in one year. New roles, new departments, and new people.

While an all-virtual workplace is efficient, our newer employees didn't really know their coworkers very well. Existing employees needed to rekindle relationships based on new roles and interactions. We needed to *know* each other better.

As Chief Human Resources Officer, I was busy getting the organization ready to grow, but that wasn't as straightforward as we assumed it would be. After a bumpy transition year, the easy answer seemed to be, "Let's have an all-employee meeting in person!" And for most leaders and HR pros, that's where the thinking ends and the logistics of event planning begins.

But having an in-person meeting for the sake of being in-person didn't make sense. Getting employees together is expensive, seems contrary to an all-virtual work environment, and disrupts the daily cadence of working from home, a key reason employees decided to work at CoachSource.

NOT YOUR TYPICAL EMPLOYEE MEETING

I took a pause in my "all-employee meeting" thinking and decided to create an intentional gathering. I met with our C-suite team, and we created three days of intentional, in-person interactions with our core employees: the C-suite, account management teams, and support staff. These were the people who could solve the current business and culture dilemmas. We crafted a team gathering for thirty people at a hotel that followed this schedule:

Day 1: C-suite meeting to finalize and clearly articulate strategic priorities.

Day 2: Vice presidents joining the C-suite team to align on strategic priorities, and Mary Dombrowski, the Senior Vice President of Client Engagement, meeting with account teams to share the growth strategy.

Day 3: All-team meeting to strengthen relationships, deepen engagement, and align around strategic priorities.

GETTING BUSINESS DONE WITH INTENTIONALITY

We were intentional about exploring, deciding, and aligning everyone as we shifted from a transition year to a year of deeper client experience and growth. During a session led by Mary Dombrowski, the account teams were concerned about the complexity of creating program proposals after an initial request from clients. I could see the frustration in the faces of the account teams as they shared this challenge. That's when Mary said, "You don't need to send anything after the first request!"

I watched their faces relax, their shoulders release tension and drop down, and several of them let out an audible sigh of relief! Whew!

"Here are four questions and conversations to have before you decide to send anything to the client," Mary continued, and then she shared a solution that made everyone's jobs easier to perform.

Our intentional interactions by unpacking this dilemma in person sparked the solution for everyone and created a shared experience that changed the way they worked together going forward.

DEEPENING RELATIONSHIPS WITH INTENTIONALITY

We were intentional about cultivating culture and relationships, too. I surveyed employees prior to our gathering, asking what they wanted to experience, and the response was a resounding, "Time to socialize and get to know each other better!"

I created thirty-minute breaks on the agenda and mealtimes longer than one hour. We started each day mid-morning so employees could exercise together in the hotel gym, meet for coffee, or take walks. Since I'm a professional speaker, I served as emcee, presented sessions, and incorporated lots of humor and games into the schedule that helped employees learn more about each other while having fun.

We hosted a dinner at Brian Underhill's home. Brian and his wife created an atmosphere that was like a welcoming party for new employees and a reunion for existing employees. We sat for dinner together at one long table that extended through the dining room, living room, and foyer. I sat at one end of the table and marveled at the variety of lively conversations and laughter occurring up and down the table. People were learning about their colleagues' hobbies, pets, families, friends, and their interests outside of work. The dinner sparked new relationships and deepened existing relationships.

Our three-day gathering achieved the specific intentions of each interaction and positioned everyone to be more engaged in and prepared for the pursuit of our company-wide goals.

CRAFTING INTENTIONAL INTERACTIONS

Now it's your turn to craft intentional interactions. Every gathering and interaction is contextual. Know the context of your organization, people, culture, and business needs. Then craft intentional interactions to achieve the outcomes that fit your context. Here are some best practices as you craft intentional interactions.

- **Where You Gather Matters, but It Doesn't Need to Be Fancy or Expensive.** You don't need a fancy skyscraper with sweeping city views to woo candidates during final interviews. Select a conversation space that's quiet, relaxing, and puts the candidate at ease. Team gatherings don't need to be in expensive hotels. Select a location that fosters interaction and conversations. Our CoachSource gathering was in a modest hotel, and we decorated the meeting space with old company banners and exhibit displays to showcase how far we've progressed since our inception. The hotel was next door to an outdoor shopping and dining complex, allowing for easy access to dinners and social activities for small or large groups. Make it easy for people to get outside the meeting room and socialize.

CRAFTING INTENTIONAL INTERACTIONS AT WORK

- **Meet People at the Door.** Meeting new employees at Humana's front door was more than just good logistics. It was a personable, warm interaction that set the tone of the workplace as one of belonging and engagement. Let your face be the first one they see before reception or security. For CoachSource's gathering, we knew employees would travel and arrive at various times before meetings began, so we notified employees to gather in the lobby at specific times so people could welcome each other and meet with intention.

- **Eat Together.** Food brings people together. At Humana, having lunch together in the company's cafeteria was more than convenient: it was a conversation focused on the interaction without the complications of going out to a restaurant. At CoachSource's gathering, we intentionally created a variety of ways to eat together. Some meals were "on your own" at the various restaurants next door to the hotel. Some were served in our meeting room to maximize our gathering time. We hosted a dinner at Brian's home to make use of an intentionally warm, welcoming space that brought us together at one table.

- **Take Long Breaks.** I understand why meeting planners minimize hotel meeting days to save money. Most conferences I've attended start at 7:00 AM and end at 7:30 PM! It is humanly impossible to muster the energy or attention to be productive or intentional for twelve hours. You've probably had meaningful, enjoyable conversations between conference sessions during breaks, at meals, and after the meeting day ends. Create breaks that are at least thirty minutes or longer and give people time to linger. Trust me on this one. Take. Long. Breaks.

- **Be Intentional about Whom to Invite—and Whom *Not* to Invite.** I know this sounds exclusive and elitist, but including everyone without an intention is not useful, and it's expensive. I learned this from Priya Parker's book, *The Art* *of Gathering: How We Meet and Why It Matters.* If you take the time to craft the intention, purpose, and expected outcome of an interview, new employee onboarding, project team meeting, or company event, it will be easier to determine who needs to participate and who does not. This ensures that your gathering accomplishes its purpose.

At Humana, we decided that only one member of the team needed to meet the new employee at the front door on their first day. Duets and trios of the team took the new employee to lunch. Another member of the team helped with office equipment.

At CoachSource, the first day only required the C-suite team to finalize strategic intentions, while it was critical to add the vice presidents on the second day to engage them for the year's intentions.

- **Watch for Signals That Intentional Interactions Are Occurring.** You've done all the intentional planning, so now, watch for signals during the gathering that your intentions are working—or if they're not working—so you can adjust in the moment.

At Humana, the signal that meeting new employees at the front door was working as intended was the expressions of surprise and relief on their faces when they saw their new coworker waiting for them. Another signal was the lobby conversations that put the new employee at ease. We allowed time for the employee to relax instead of whisking them to security to get their badge.

At CoachSource, we scheduled gatherings in the hotel lobby as employees arrived from their travel day. I knew these were working when I saw the smiles of employees and the hugs between them when meeting each other for the first time, witnessing them engaging in conversations and planning impromptu dinners on their own. During dinner at Brian's home, I knew the intentions were working as people expressed surprise and curiosity when they learned more about their coworkers, when bursts of laughter were heard up and down the table, and when people were disappointed when the evening came to an end.

CREATE INTENTIONAL INTERACTIONS FOR YOUR TEAM AND ORGANIZATION

Ask yourself, "What are the intentional interactions, workspaces, and environments that inspired and engaged me?" Can you picture them? What did people *do* to make you feel valued or accelerate the outcome of gathering in person? What did you *see* that engaged you? What did you *smell* that helped you recall the interaction? What did you *hear* that deepened your conversation, understanding, or connection with other people? What did you *touch or feel* that connected you to the space? And what did you *experience* that did *not* generate intentional interactions so you know what *not* to do?

Now more than ever, humans at work are starving for deeper, more meaningful interactions outside the video conference screen.

Use those memories and what you learned in this chapter to craft your next intentional interaction, so your team and organization can be more engaged, perform at higher levels, and deepen relationships. Implement the examples and recommendations, and experience the results. And let me hear from you! Please visit https://www.nallygroup.com/whenworkworks/ to share what's working for you, to learn from your peers, and to use more resources to create intentional interactions.

Now more than ever, humans at work are starving for deeper, more meaningful interactions outside the video conference screen. Whatever the gathering space, let's not forget *why* we bring human beings to work together and *where* they gather. It matters. It's meaningful. And intentional interactions work.

Chapter 12

All Guts? No Glory: Stop Relying on Referrals, Gut Feel, and Luck to Hire Top Talent

Amy Oviedo

Founder, Recruiting Experiences

recruitingexperiences.com

linkedin.com/in/amyoviedo

linkedin.com/company/recruitingex

facebook.com/RecruitingExperiences

Amy Oviedo is a recruitment consultant, speaker, and trainer who founded and leads Recruiting Experiences. She focuses on bringing process, data, and kindness to the recruiting world. Amy has completed over 30,000 interviews throughout her career and personally recruited and hired over 2,500 professionals.

Amy's career spans multiple industries and she especially enjoys working with technology start-up and scale-up organizations, high-volume recruiting teams, not-for-profit organizations, and scarce talent pools. She develops and delivers an accredited Talent Acquisition Professional Certification to help anyone looking to expand their recruiting skills. She specializes in enhancing interview skills, eliminating bias in talent acquisition, using AI to drive results through people, and delivering positive candidate experiences.

Amy's organization, Recruiting Experiences, offers flat-fee professional recruitment services, fractional HR services, talent consulting, and training opportunities. Designed to operate as an extension of your brand, consult with your team, and find hidden talent, Recruiting Experiences is not just another recruiting firm.

• • •

I graduated from college without a career plan. I flipped a coin and ended up on my sister's couch in Chicago. I found a job through a temp agency by answering a newspaper ad. Starting at a global company in benefits administration, I was bored to tears. The woman across from me was the company's sole recruiter. Her job was so much better than mine. After ten months, I found another ad in the paper for my new dream job—a commission-only recruiter position at a company founded by two minority women. They had resigned from a nationwide firm to grow something of their own. Two independent, young women starting a business was simply unheard of at that time.

Day 1

I arrived at the company's downtown office, which was on the 34th floor of a high-rise, and found my new boss in her closet-sized office. She walked me to my desk—which was about six steps away.

There were four desks in the "bullpen," arranged like those in a kindergarten classroom. I sat directly across from my fellow newbie. We introduced ourselves and were told to "settle in."

Four desks. Four chairs. Four phones. Four yellow legal pads. Two phone books. Two bosses. One computer. Settling in, I grabbed a pen and my padfolio. It was 1998, and I was about to get schooled in old-school recruiting!

Boss #2 arrived with two newspapers—the *Chicago Sun Times* and the *Tribune*. She advised us to get acquainted with the "Help Wanted" section. These are not the words you expect to hear on your first day at your dream job! At 10:05 am, we began training, starting with the newspapers. The instructions were simple:

1. Read ads. Circle anything that sounds like technology.
2. Look up the company contact in the phone book... yep, the "yellow pages."
3. Call the company. Ask for IT. Be kind to the receptionist.
4. Do what it takes to get the name of the decision-maker and get transferred.
5. When you get someone in IT on the phone, ask if they use agencies. Yes? Proceed.
6. Tell them you are an experienced recruiter and your firm has made several placements of whatever title they advertised. Negotiate the opportunity to work on their jobs at a contingent rate—no pay unless you fill the job.

This seemingly chaotic process worked for me at least once a day. Each of our managers did two demo calls on speaker that morning and handed us the phones. By 11 AM, we had been "fully trained" in Sales! I was too naïve to realize I should be terrified, so I started dialing. We made calls until they suggested we go get some lunch. I never saw my new coworker again.

The afternoon schedule was recruitment training. We learned sales in two hours, so this should be easy! Boss #2 said she had some interviews lined up and needed to call clients to check the progress of her candidates. In the meantime, she instructed me to make a list of everyone I knew. This was in 1998—we're five years from the launch of LinkedIn, and six years before Facebook. I didn't even have a cell phone!

"Write down the names and start finding phone numbers of every person you know. You'll need them later."

I did this for the rest of the day while eavesdropping on phone calls.

Day 2

I was the first to arrive and settle into my desk, grabbing the *Sun-Times* off my former coworker's desk. Two hours into cold calls, someone said "yes!" I took an order for a Sybase DBA. Sybase was an early version of database technology similar to Microsoft's SQL and would be bought by SAP in 2010.

I was shocked that someone had agreed to let me recruit for their position. So were my new bosses. Boss #1 told me that Sybase roles are impossible to fill. Her advice? Keep making sales calls for the morning and then continue adding onto my list of everyone I know in the afternoon. I nodded. I'm learning. I'll follow the path. I didn't get any other hits that day. I continued the task of listing everyone I've ever known. I call my Mom to gather phone numbers and then head out around 6:45 PM. I can't wait to get home to my computer and start researching. I hadn't been offered use of the office computer. Yahoo, here I come!

Yahoo Search Bar: how to recruit IT workers

Results: HotJobs, Dice, CareerBuilder, Monster, Headhunter.net

Day 3

I went in early to catch Boss #1 and ask if she's considered buying access to an online resume database. She said I need to build my own candidate leads, indicating her yellow legal pad. She went on to say that, if I want to research it, she's open to suggestions. Monster.com had launched in 1996, so all of these options had been in the market for less than two years – tough sell!

"From what I've learned so far, I'd like to consider HotJobs and Monster. Okay to set up demos?"

She agreed, and we ended up purchasing HotJobs.com access a week later. While Boss #2 called everyone she knew and got referrals, I called strangers from HotJobs and asked them for referrals.

Generally, my morning sales calls resulted in one "yes" each day. Boss #2 submitted some candidates to a few of my jobs from her network, while I worked to master online search and my referral strategy. At night, I accessed HotJobs and AOL chat groups from home, working on the Sybase role I'm not supposed to work on. I find two viable candidates and submit them. The hiring manager calls me immediately to request interviews. After scheduling, I tell Boss #2 what I've been doing with my evenings. She looks proud; definitely not mad!

In three weeks, I've created some traction and was excited for my candidates to complete in-person interviews. I got a call just after the second one. My client wanted to offer one of my candidates the job! I was in shock, but still acted like a recruiter who's done this a bunch of times. I asked about salary and we agreed to the number I recommended. I asked when they wanted him to start and about next steps. I hung up and immediately called the candidate to share the good news. He verbally accepted! At this point, my bosses have gathered by my desk to listen. They were in shock, too!

"Where did you find that guy?"

"How did you know what salary to offer?"

"How did you know to ask when he could start?"

"What did they say?"

I smiled and flipped my yellow pad to a process flow I've been jotting down while listening to Boss #2 make calls each afternoon. I knew my list of "everyone I know" wasn't going to have the right candidates, so I was looking for alternate paths. I found one of the candidates on HotJobs and got a referral to the new hire in an AOL chat room.

The candidate called me on his first day to thank me—he loved his new boss and was excited about the work. My first commission covered my $7.50 per hour draw in full and I got a $7,200 commission check. I am hooked on recruiting—the thrill of the chase, the satisfaction of a match, and I can pay my rent!

What I learned over the next several years is that old-school, relationship-based recruiting works in some circumstances. The core process of candidate outreach, hiring team management, interviewing, and offer negotiation are similar whether you're reaching out to acquaintances or strangers. Companies' desire to continuously hire top talent and build a pipeline of future talent, alongside making advances in technology and human communication, has heightened the necessity for updated methods and a more robust, repeatable recruiting process.

CAST A NET BEYOND YOUR REFERRALS

Casting a wide net has almost always paid off for me in recruiting and is a regular part of my recruiting process. This strategy uncovers candidates who wouldn't have been in my initial call list of "everyone I know" written out on a legal pad, or even today's version of this, 15K+ connections on LinkedIn. The first step in any recruiting process, after narrowing down requirements and all the basics of the role, such as location and hours, is to develop a sourcing strategy. Referrals will be part of the strategy. Getting beyond "who you know" can be challenging for some hiring teams, and it is critical for long-term success.

Getting beyond "who you know" can be challenging for some hiring teams, and it is critical for long-term success.

Start-ups and scale-ups are notorious for hiring referrals during high-growth phases, which can lead to homogenous work environments. If everyone being hired is referred by your team, candidates are likely to have similar backgrounds, work experiences, or education credentials. One of the tech companies I worked for early in my career hired 80% of their sales professionals based on referrals or from the same university. When I shared my concerns with the CEO and VP of Sales, I was allowed to bring in new pools of candidates to interview alongside the traditional candidates—referrals and graduates of their shared alma mater. When my direct-sourced candidates weren't selected, job criteria was rarely mentioned to explain hiring one candidate over another.

I have nothing against referrals. That being said, there are multiple ways to find qualified candidates. After a year of agency recruiting, an acquaintance referred me to a tech scale-up hiring their first recruiter. One year of experience landed me an internal recruiting gig, and I quickly learned referrals often tended to be the least qualified candidates for the company's roles. Knowing someone at the company can help you ace the interview, but it won't change your qualifications. I was not qualified for the role simply because my acquaintance, an accountant, remembered I was a recruiter after meeting me at karaoke!

Despite the evidence to support diversifying both teams and source of hires, referrals remain a strong draw for many hiring managers. A 2016 Harvard Business Review article reports companies with more diverse teams are, on average, 35% more productive than their more homogenous counterparts. They also net 250% more cash flow and report higher annual profits. Moving the industry beyond the 30-35% referrals hired each year is critical for expanding team capabilities and company success.

A solid search strategy will incorporate components of inbound applicant traffic and outbound sourcing tactics. Developing a sourcing plan for each hire will increase quality candidate flow and make the difference in expanding your reach beyond referrals.

YOUR GUT BETRAYS YOU

I worked with a CEO known for clever phrases. One he repeated often was, "Don't trust your gut. Obey it."

While the phrase is memorable, our gut instincts are often wrong. Sure, we remember the times we got it right and everything worked out. I'm not proposing regret or looking back. Yet, we can learn from our missteps. Think of all the times your gut was not quite right. I bet your list is as long as mine!

The heart of the debate is this: Interviewers inherently bring bias to the process. Our brains are wired for bias. We take information we've learned in the past and use it to predict future behaviors. Much like our prehistoric ancestors, we know when and where the saber-toothed tiger is likely to strike and we avoid those paths. It's natural for past hiring mistakes to bias future interview interactions.

Three main types of bias occur in recruiting most often: halo effect, horn effect, and affinity bias. The halo and horn effects describe our bias in assigning positive and negative traits to new candidates based on similarities between the candidate background and past hire profiles. Affinity bias, on the other hand, attributes our own successes and failures to aspects of our personal background, which may align to a candidate profile. Individuals are naturally drawn to people similar to them.

Knowing our bias allows us to control it. Awareness reminds us to pause and think, *do I know this to be true?* Encountering a resume with a degree from a university you attended or have an affinity for often creates a positive bias. We may even overlook negative traits uncovered during the interview. In the same way, if the candidate graduated from your university's rival, you may unknowingly look for negative traits to confirm your bias. Sometimes our biases are less blatant. For example, if you had an internship experience at a retail organization, you may value retail experience more highly compared to an interviewer who has never worked in retail and doesn't see how it could be adequate preparation for a corporate role.

One of my current clients, a SAAS provider with thirty employees, invested in their training and recruiting process early in their hiring journey. The CEO was determined to build a team with shared values who would respect and honor the culture he envisioned. By focusing heavily on hiring talent who identified with the culture, the team has experienced only two separations in their first ten years—remarkable results derived from a scalable, value-first recruitment process.

A highly impactful exercise for leadership teams to engage in is interview training. By learning to interview using a structured process that allows for the identification of top talent and evaluation of job criteria from an unbiased position, organizations can consistently find top talent while scaling their business. Teams can learn to structure their interviews to assess skills, competencies, and values, rather than relying on gut feelings.

Bottom line: Learn what biases you bring to the process.

Bottom line: Learn what biases you bring to the process. Pause and reflect on the actual traits identified in the interview to make your decision without the inherent bias you will undoubtedly encounter.

LUCK IS NOT A STRATEGY

I consider myself a lucky person. I believe I win random contests more often than others. I believe in the power of karma—putting good into the world comes back to you. I also believe in process, data, and hard work. None of us are one-dimensional, and our processes should not be one-dimensional, either.

Creating a process doesn't mean luck won't be on your side. Meeting the right co-founder or finding the right sales leader can be serendipitous for many organizations. Relying on these opportunities, however, is not a strategy. Creating processes based on past success and market data is critical to applying the building blocks toward success.

When I was managing a $1M recruiting budget for a large hospitality provider, I used data to evaluate what was working and make spending decisions. For example, we were spending a large amount on a particular job board, and while about 6% of our hires were coming from that resource, we also found that over 50% of our applicants were coming from there. Evaluating only one data point showed that the tons of applicants justified the expense. The real question was: How much time were we losing evaluating unqualified applicants? Digging deeper, I found our lower spend categories were getting equal or better hiring impact without drawing large numbers of unqualified applicants. Continual evaluation of our data allowed better budget decisions without sacrificing hiring results.

Recruiting is a lot like Sales. Where it often differs is in opinions from all stakeholders. If I sold cars, the vehicle would have no opinion about being sold. In recruiting, the candidate and all members of the hiring team have opinions about the result. It is my job, as a recruiter, aided by the hiring team, to understand the needs of all parties and negotiate on behalf of each party to find common ground. Ultimately, an offer being accepted by the selected candidate is the desired outcome. Getting there while advocating for both sides and ensuring neither party is giving more than needed to find a great match is an art—often with a side of luck. Timing, spousal or familial input, counteroffers, and any myriad of other factors can influence the final answer. Anticipating and addressing these needs is the hallmark of a great recruiter. Getting ahead of potential questions and concerns allows both the candidate and the hiring manager to feel confident in their decision to move forward.

WHERE DO I START IN BUILDING A VALUABLE RECRUITING PROCESS?

Start slow. Choose two to three parts of your process you wish to improve immediately. A recruiting process is made up of several components: employer brand; technology; job descriptions; marketing; sourcing strategies; hiring team collaboration;

candidate experience and communication; screening and interviewing; selection; negotiation; offers; and the ability to pivot when needed. Tackling all of them at once is overwhelming.

If you have not defined a process at all, start by helping hiring managers identify the "must-have" and "nice-to-have" skills for each role. You can then create compelling job descriptions and interview questions to guide candidate discussions. If you have some process in place already, continue reviewing data inputs and outcomes. Identify what is working and areas of improvement by asking new hires and managers for their input. Work with hiring teams and recruiters to solidify commitments to the process consistently. Training hiring teams and ensuring everyone is committed to positive hiring outcomes is always a great place to start.

Your gut will betray you sometimes. Hiring too many referrals creates stagnant environments. Luck will only sometimes be on your side. A process with measurable results allows you to build a more productive, diverse, and impactful team. With so many tools available to today's recruiters, maintaining focus on a repeatable recruiting process can make the difference in attracting and retaining top talent. Work *works* when the right talent is on board.

The lesson I learned sharing my yellow pad process with my bosses in 1998 was lost on me at that moment. It struck me once more in 2021 as I was developing a talent acquisition certification program. Process was my catalyst for a successful career in recruiting, and I've seen it change the game for so many companies. Embracing the process and structuring a scalable recruiting platform provides a competitive advantage to organizations building for their future.

Download my checklist, "Recruiting with Impact," at www.recruitingexperiences.com/whenworkworks.

Chapter 13

Empowering the Frontline: When Work Works for Those Who Matter Most

Molley Ricketts

CEO & Founder of Incipio Workforce Solutions

incipioworks.com

facebook.com/IncipioWorks

linkedin.com/in/molleyricketts

Molley Ricketts, CEO of Incipio Workforce Solutions (incipioworks.com), started to support small- to medium-sized companies with recruitment, retention, HR support, workforce alignment, employer branding, and outplacement services. Over years of supporting companies, she saw employers' need to understand the value of an engaged workforce. For the last nine years, Incipio Workforce Solutions has been doing just that for companies in the Kentuckiana area and all over the U.S. During the previous four years, they have focused on essential workers' impact on the manufacturing, healthcare, and hospitality industries.

Born and raised in Louisville, KY, Molley married her high school sweetheart, Chad, and they have raised two fantastic adult children and contributing members of society in their hometown. When she is not working, Molley loves to be surrounded by family and friends anywhere close to the water, but their second home at Lake Cumberland, Kentucky, is where they can often be found. Molley and her husband, Chad, also have a fun podcast, *Lake Life with Molley and Chad*, where they share their love of lake life with others; it's now in its fourth season and currently on all podcast listening platforms.

• • •

Frontline workers, essential workers, entry-level workers, deskless workers, mid-level manager and staff positions: this category of employee continues to be surprisingly undervalued even after the global pandemic. During that tumultuous time, these employees still had to show up and do the work. Every day. These are the unsung heroes, the **essential workers**.

Who are these "essential workers?" Why are they important to so many organizations? And how can employers make a difference in their employment experience and, ultimately, their lives?

An essential worker typically provides vital services that cannot be interrupted without severe consequences or significant disruptions to public health, safety, or well-being. Essential workers include healthcare professionals, construction workers, manufacturing workers, emergency responders, law enforcement officers, grocery store employees, sanitation workers, public transportation operators, utility workers, and others who perform essential functions to keep communities running smoothly. A strong essential worker community is imperative for maintaining the functioning of society and the economy, especially during times of crisis. Recognizing the importance of these workers and providing them with adequate support, resources, and protections are crucial for ensuring resilience and stability in the face of everyday and once-in-a-lifetime challenges.

A myriad of factors underlie the inaccurate valuation of the essential worker: underappreciation of labor, economic inequality, social status and perception, lack of recognition, to name a few. The devaluation of essential workers is a complex issue rooted in societal attitudes, economic structures, and power dynamics.

Recognizing and addressing these factors is vital for ensuring that all workers are treated with the respect and dignity they deserve.

Many essential workers perform jobs that are vitally important to society's functioning but remain undervalued and underpaid. These jobs are often seen as low-skilled, despite their critical importance. Essential workers—especially in sectors like healthcare, construction, manufacturing, retail, and food service—often face low wages, lack of benefits, and job insecurity. This economic inequality contributes to the perception that these workers are somehow less important or less valuable. There can be a societal bias against certain types of work, leading to the devaluation of those who perform these integral roles.

Jobs that involve manual labor, service work, or caregiving are sometimes viewed as less prestigious than roles in fields like technology or finance. Essential workers may not receive the recognition and respect they deserve for their contributions, especially during times of crisis. While they are crucial for maintaining indispensable services, their work may go unnoticed or unacknowledged by those who benefit from it. Power dynamics within society and the workplace can also play a role. Those in positions of power may not fully appreciate or understand the challenges faced by essential workers, leading to decisions that prioritize other interests over the well-being of these workers.

It's a sad reality that essential workers often bear the brunt of demanding roles, all while not receiving the support they require for their well-being. Their dedication is truly commendable, as they serve as the backbone of America's infrastructure. This underscores how concerning it is that many of them are less likely to willingly seek or receive support.

It's crucial for employers and communities to recognize the importance of prioritizing the mental and physical health of frontline workers and to provide accessible avenues for support and resources. This could include offering counseling services, implementing wellness programs, and fostering a supportive work environment that encourages open dialogue about well-being.

Without recognizing the value of a strong essential worker community, businesses will rise only to fall. Look at the employee landscape post-pandemic to see how many essential workers left their employers for more money, better working environments, access to medical benefits, a less stressful environment, or new educational opportunities.

WHY ARE THESE ESSENTIAL WORKERS SO VITAL?

Public Health Impact. A breakdown in essential services could lead to worsened public health outcomes. For example, without adequate healthcare workers, hospitals may struggle to provide necessary medical care, leading to increased illness and mortality rates.

Economic Slowdown. Disruptions in essential services can have a cascading effect on the broader economy. For instance, if transportation networks are disrupted, it could lead to delays in the delivery of goods, impacting businesses across various sectors and causing economic downturns.

Increased Vulnerability to Crises. A weak essential worker community leaves society more vulnerable to crises and emergencies, whether they be natural disasters, pandemics, or other unforeseen events. Without a robust workforce to respond to such crises, the ability to recover and rebuild would be severely compromised.

Social Unrest. Inadequate support for essential workers can lead to dissatisfaction, labor strikes, or protests, potentially resulting in social unrest and instability. This could further exacerbate economic challenges and hinder efforts to address underlying issues.

THE STRUGGLES OF ESSENTIAL WORKERS

Today we are facing an almost unprecedented employment crisis. The employment crisis affects many individuals, including both adult and dislocated workers. Adult workers, typically those aged twenty-five and older, may face challenges related to housing, transportation, childcare, layoffs, reduced hours, or finding stable employment. Dislocated workers are individuals who have lost their jobs due to company closures, mass layoffs, or other economic factors beyond their control.

During employment crises, both groups often struggle to find new employment opportunities or reenter the workforce because their current skills are no longer relevant. They may also face obstacles such as illiteracy, basic computer skills, lack of education or training for in-demand fields, and limited access to resources for job searching and career development.

Efforts to support adult and dislocated workers during employment crises often involve retraining programs, job placement assistance, financial aid, and other resources to help them transition into new roles or industries. Smart business owners may collaborate with government and non-profit organizations to provide these resources to underutilized "potential" employees. Forward-thinking business owners will be on the cutting edge by stabilizing their workforce through new job creation that demonstrates concern for their employees' well-being while building brand loyalty, increasing employee retention, and increasing bottom-line profitability. Now that's a win-win-win!

WHAT SHOULD CONTEMPORARY WORKPLACES PROVIDE FOR ESSENTIAL WORKERS?

As a forward-thinking employer, you will want to create an environment that values essential workers' contributions, prioritizes their well-being, and gives them the support and resources they need to thrive in their roles. When work truly works for essential workers, you recognize their humanity, respect their contributions, and prioritize their well-being in the following areas.

Safe Working Conditions: Ensuring a safe work environment is crucial. Employers should provide necessary protective gear, enforce safety protocols, and regularly assess and address any risks to employee health and safety.

Fair Compensation: Essential workers should receive fair compensation for their work, including wages that reflect the value of their contributions to society. This may include hazard pay or other incentives during times of increased risk.

Opportunities for Advancement: Essential workers should have opportunities for career growth and development. This can include access to training programs, educational opportunities, and pathways to higher-paying positions within their field.

Work-Life Balance: Try to provide essential workers with reasonable hours and schedules that allow for adequate rest and time with their families. This can help prevent burnout and maintain mental and physical well-being.

Access to Benefits: Essential workers should have access to healthcare benefits, including medical insurance and paid sick leave, to ensure they can take care of their own health and well-being without financial strain.

Recognition and Appreciation: Essential workers should be recognized and appreciated for their contributions to society, both by their employers and by the broader community. This can help boost morale and job satisfaction. Recognizing the vital contribution of essential workers goes beyond mere words. Employers and society at large should show appreciation through tangible actions, such as providing bonuses, offering awards, or organizing events to celebrate their efforts.

Supportive Work Culture: Fostering a supportive work culture is crucial for the well-being of essential workers. This involves promoting teamwork, fostering open communication, and providing resources for mental health support.

Community Support: Beyond the workplace, communities should also support essential workers. This can include initiatives such as providing discounts, offering free services, or simply expressing gratitude for their contributions.

Training and Development: Essential workers should have access to training and opportunities for professional development to enhance their skills and advance their careers. This increases job satisfaction while also helping avoid the common pitfall of promotion to failure in this class of worker. Without development, a strongly performing worker who is rewarded with a promotion will not be prepared, which results in them facing an increased chance of failure in their new role.

Voice and Representation: Essential workers should have a voice in decisions that affect their work and should be represented in discussions about workplace policies and conditions. This can happen through employee councils, team meetings, or other forms of representation.

REIMAGINING WORK IN DOLLARS AND SENSE

Chances are, if you could hire workers more quickly and effectively than you can now, your organization would grow. Workers would have more higher-wage opportunities if you could better match workers with jobs by placing workers in roles that best fit their strengths and aspirations. Makes sense, doesn't it?

With the reinvention of the US economy will come a reimagining of how leaders think about talent. How do we assess learning styles for essential workers? How do we best combine in-person, digital, and virtual training for essential workers? How do businesses best reward workers who train others? How do we create career paths across industries so that workers don't view entry-level jobs as dead-ends but as stepping stones to a better life? How do we transition AI-displaced desktop workers to essential work?

It is critical that you consider the ways essential workers directly impact your overall cost of operating. Emphasizing the importance of recognizing, supporting, and empowering essential workers has the potential to inspire meaningful action and drive positive outcomes. A truly engaged essential worker is fully committed to their work, motivated to excel, and deeply connected to their organization's mission and goals. The benefits of having engaged essential workers are plentiful and should be a focus for employers and community leaders.

Engaged essential workers are more likely to be focused and dedicated to their tasks, leading to increased productivity and efficiency in their roles. This engagement creates improved quality of their work output, which leads to higher productivity, which leads to increasing profitability. Engagement also inspires a strong sense of pride, which is evident in delivery of services. This difference is highly perceptible, as employees go the extra mile to delight customers, leading to improved customer satisfaction and brand loyalty. Individuals foster innovation within the organization to contribute ideas and solutions, improving processes, which, again, is another way to reduce cost and increase revenues.

MEASURING THE RETURN ON INVESTMENT (ROI) FOR ESSENTIAL WORKERS

If the bottom line of all successful businesses is to reduce cost and increase revenue, then you need to understand how much it costs to attract, onboard, and assimilate individuals to your company to the point they are making money for your company, not costing your company money. This phase is called *churn*, and it costs approximately $7,000 per "Day One" employee.

The next major cost of hiring essential workers is *turnover*. Turnover follows churn as the point after the organization has invested in training, supplies, supervised support, and so on, to ready the employee to produce on the investment that's been made in them thus far. Between the costs of churn and turnover, a company can spend thousands of dollars and still have a weak workforce. If employers don't spend adequate time truly investing in meeting the needs of their essential workers' well-being, the organization may ultimately fail. Many employers are resigned to or erroneously categorize this expense as a "cost of doing business," when it can be improved and remedied by placing proper value on the essential worker.

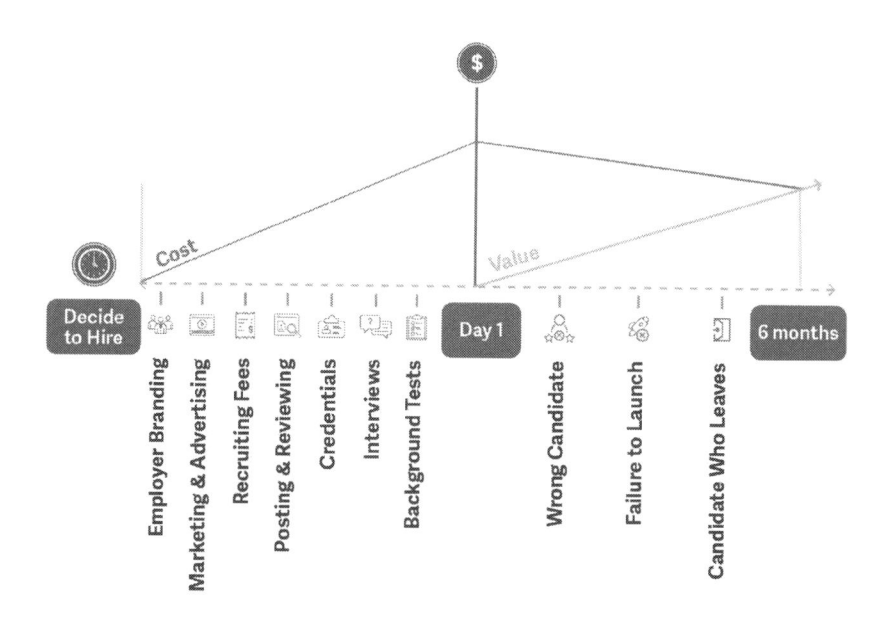

Lowering churn and turnover will support the engaged essential workers. Providing stable and satisfactory employment for people that allows them to enjoy their work, see the value that they are adding, and build comradery within their teams makes them less likely to seek employment elsewhere. This reduces turnover rates and the associated costs of recruitment and training. Workers contribute more to a positive work culture characterized by teamwork, collaboration, and mutual respect, which can boost morale and overall job satisfaction. When you have this level of satisfaction during times of crisis or uncertainty, engaged essential workers are more likely to remain committed and adaptable, helping the organization navigate challenges effectively. Having engaged essential workers is paramount for organizational success, as they play a crucial role in driving performance, fostering innovation, and maintaining a positive workplace culture.

A CASE STUDY

A manufacturing company that I've worked with has experienced ongoing success and keeps growing because they are focusing on the "total" employee. A sustainable food-grade manufacturing company approached me with the hiring pains they were experiencing at multiple manufacturing locations across the Midwest. Along with many other organizations and industries, their organization needed help with:

- Talent acquisition
- Lowering turnover rates
- Community engagement
- Employer branding
- Onboarding and training processes
- Creating a positive workplace culture

This organization recognized the need for a comprehensive solution, and my team was able to transform their hiring efforts in three years, reshape their employer brand, and create a healthy organizational culture that impacted retention. Each portion of the engagement, from employer branding to recruitment to workforce alignment, played an integral role in reaching the overall goal and objective of attracting and hiring the right people for the right positions, retaining them, and building a culture they never wanted to leave.

Before our partnership, this organization suffered from a toxic management style that tarnished their reputation. While recruiting and employer branding were helping with this transformational change, we all agreed a long-term culture shift was needed. My team nurtured all training and continuous feedback efforts with the client's internal team. Through a custom-made survey tool, we diagnosed the pain points that caused high turnover for the manufacturer. Their employees felt overwhelmed by the lack of solid training to succeed in their operator roles.

This holistic approach aimed to provide a seamless transition for new hires, from the initial onboarding process to long-term integration within the company. By empowering their employees and aligning them with the company's vision, we helped this organization achieve greater operational efficiency, reduce the cost of turnover, and recognize an improvement in their retention rates, thereby decreasing costs and increasing revenues! Talk about "raving fans!"

THE GOLDEN NUGGET

Now, for the golden nugget! How do successful organizations lower their operating costs and increase revenues by creating an engaged workforce? Quite simply, they ask their employees! Employers who ask employees what they want and need to create and maintain a positive work environment are employers who likely have a highly engaged workforce. This is not astrophysics! This is understanding that every person needs to feel valued and respected so they can contribute in a meaningful way to the greater good. Essential workers want to contribute, but societal perspectives often diminish them. These are the very people who keep our country running every single day! Isn't that quite a paradox?

Conducting carefully-crafted employee engagement surveys is the most effective way to ask specific questions that provide leaders with information they can use to build a desirable culture that meets the needs of essential workers.

Over the last nine years, we've partnered with multiple companies in numerous industries that employ essential workers. Creating a short employee survey and receiving the responses openly empowers organizations to encourage clear and candid communication between management and employees. It is instrumental to listen to employee concerns, provide feedback, and keep employees informed about company goals and changes.

Showing your commitment to the workforce by implementing changes that are a direct result of the surveys will foster an immediate change in the environment, giving employees proof that their opinions matter. As a result, value, motivation, and connection happen. By establishing a culture of continuous feedback, where employees feel comfortable providing and receiving constructive feedback, areas for improvement can be identified and issues addressed before they escalate.

I've continually witnessed how investing in strong leadership inspires trust and confidence while providing stability and belonging. Leaders should be approachable, supportive, and capable of guiding their teams effectively. Organize team-building activities and social events to foster camaraderie and strengthen relationships among employees. Ensure that employees understand how their work contributes to the overall goals and success of the company. Help them find purpose and meaning in their roles.

Wise leaders are laser-focused on making this a priority in the essential worker employment experience. Empower your leaders to take ownership of their projects and initiatives. You will see success in defining meaningful work. By implementing these strategies, you can create an engaged workforce that is more likely to stay with the company long term, thus reducing turnover rates.

You can do it.

You must do it.

The future of the economy depends on employers changing the way they employ people, considering and enhancing the way their employees live. Ultimately, this results in a community that brings value not only to the essential worker's workplace but also to their world. And we can all agree that living in a place that provides stability and belonging is a win for us all!

Chapter 14

"So, What Do You Do?": The Answer Your CEO Will Love!

S. Richard Park, Ph.D.

Principal - Talent Alignment, LLC

🌐 talentalignment.net
in linkedin.com/in/rickpark

Rick Park partners with executive business leaders to create a competitive advantage through people. He has held specialized roles in assessment design and validation, workforce development, rewards, performance management, culture, and organizational effectiveness.

Rick's passion for business strategy prompted him to transition into HR executive roles supporting CEOs and other executives with global responsibilities. He has worked in technology (Dell, Microsoft), manufacturing (Georgia-Pacific, KSB SE & Co. KGaA), and HR consulting (AON).

Today, Rick leads an HR consulting firm called Talent Alignment, LLC. He brings a practical approach to the firm's clients by focusing on delivering a competitive advantage through people. Rick's ability to speak to executive leaders in business terms is much appreciated by his partners and their clients.

Rick earned a Ph.D. in Industrial/Organizational Psychology to help prepare him for a career in HR, talent management, and OE.

His volunteer work involves coaching incarcerated individuals and groups. He enjoys playing guitar, cycling, announcing high school sports, and home projects. He and his wife, Lisa, enjoy traveling, exploring restaurants, and spending time with their two adult children, Lauren and Michael, and their dog, Dempsey.

• • •

You're sitting next to a CEO on a plane. The two of you exchange pleasantries and chat for a while, and then the conversation turns to work. You listen to her intently as she talks about the business she leads. She has such a passion for her customers!

She ends her story with a question for you:

"So, what do you do?"

You reach into your mental filing cabinet to find a tab called "What I Do" and, without any thought, regurgitate what you find in there.

This chapter may compel you to purge your "What I Do" file and replace it with one labeled:

"I create a competitive advantage."

Read that again. The rest of this chapter assumes that this is the mindset you adopt and promote at work.

Your neighbor will be very intrigued by the "Competitive Advantage" file, so let's review what's in there.

START WITH STRATEGY

"Business strategy" is based on educated guesses about the future of a market. Executives evaluate both external factors (competitors, suppliers, customers, product substitutes, etc.) and internal factors (company competence, culture, work processes, talent, etc.) to decide how and where their business should compete.

Why "strategy" in a book about the workplace?

1. Business strategy *should* create a competitive advantage, and
2. Establishing a competitive advantage depends on the number of employees who a) understand their role in strategy execution, b) can contribute to strategy execution, and c) work diligently to do so. Plus, a good strategy.

For example, manufacturing employees will deliver a collective eye roll at "yet another 'trivial' product change" unless they know that customer needs are central to the company's strategy and customers benefit from the changes.

You start to answer your travel partner's question about your role:

"I create a competitive advantage. Establishing a competitive advantage depends on the number of employees who a) understand their role in strategy execution, b) can contribute to strategy execution, and c) work diligently to do so. Plus, a good strategy.

"My role is to partner with CEOs and other managers to help them help employees with these three things."

She asks, "Do you work in Communications?"

Establishing a competitive advantage depends on the number of employees who a) understand their role in strategy execution, b) can contribute to strategy execution, and c) work diligently to do so. Plus, a good strategy.

You respond, "Not in the traditional sense. Delivering a competitive advantage starts with breaking strategy down into what employees do and what capabilities they need to do it well. It's also important to consider the impact that culture and structure might have on employee productivity. There's more to it than speeches, meetings, and newsletters."

She hails a flight attendant, orders drinks for both of you, and with a hint of skepticism asks, "Okay, but how?"

Now she's hooked!

Most employees toss around the word "skills" to reflect the core capabilities they think incumbents need to perform a job well. But "skills" is simply too nebulous and narrow when you are faced with leveraging workforce capabilities to win in your markets. A better alternative is the *K*(nowledge), *S*(kill), *A*(bility) and *PC*(Personal Characteristics), or *KSAPC*, taxonomy:

- **K**nowledge – Learned technical facts, like the content that tax lawyers need to know about tax law.
- **S**kill – Competence gained over time, typically "hands-on" work. For example, machinists often complete multi-year apprenticeships dedicated to hands-on maintenance and repair.
- **A**bility – Mostly stable innate capabilities, like problem solving.
- **P**ersonality **C**haracteristics – Sometimes referred to as "soft skills." Collaboration and extraversion represent this category.

Job analysis is a process that experts use to catalog job activities and translate them into their underlying KSAPCs. Commonly used job analysis tactics are interviews, observations, journaling, and questionnaires.

It's important to note that conventional wisdom regarding the value of some KSAPCs does not always coincide with research.

Research on the value of "experience" shows it has no value in improving job performance. One hundred employees with two years of experience will perform no better or worse than one hundred employees with twenty.

Goleman's version of emotional intelligence is not a personal characteristic. He never meant it to function as a standalone soft skill. It's only a label that represents twelve PCs. Research has yet to establish whether some of the twelve consistently contribute to job performance (e.g. emotional self-control, positive outlook).

Back to the CEO sitting next to you. You continue...

"...Both the business and its employees are better positioned to deliver a competitive advantage when employees have a specific blend of knowledge, skills, abilities, and personal characteristics that connect to strategy."

She confirms what she's heard. "Strategy should trickle down into what employees do. What people do requires certain KSAPCs. And culture and structure influence what people do, too."

Then she asks, "How do organizations go about reinforcing this with employees?"

"Great question!" you reply. "The good news is that most organizations already have 'levers' in place to reinforce strategy-consistent behavior. You mentioned two levers already—culture and structure. Businesses also have selection, rewards, performance, and development levers to help employees help the business compete.

"Think about it like an engine with six cylinders. Organizational strategy fuels each cylinder. Each cylinder works in a different way to elicit strategy-consistent behavior from workers."

The People Engine:
Six Cylinders that Convert Strategy to Company Performance

(Diagram: Strategy funnels into an engine with six cylinders labeled Selection, Rewards, Structure, Culture, Performance, and Development, connected to a Company Performance gauge.)

"Now we're getting somewhere," says your travel partner. "Executives are like mechanics. They adjust *The People Engine* to deliver business strategy, which results in a competitive advantage."

"Exactly!" you reply. "Grab a torque wrench!"

You reach into your new mental folder labeled "I Create a Competitive Advantage" and pull out your notes on *The People Engine*. You both discuss the file's content—cylinder by cylinder.

Author's Note – Visit
https://www.talentalignment.net/thepeopleengine
for supplemental content on each cylinder.

CYLINDER 1 – SELECTION

A quick story.

Jo was tapped to launch a warehouse with the help of a consulting team. She considered the consultants' recommendations regarding technology, shelving, jobs, forklifts, etc.

After job analysis established KSAPCs for the jobs in the warehouse, the consultants bought or developed tests, role-plays, simulations, and interviews to screen candidates.

Jo's comment about the screening process after startup:

"I worried about a lot of things while we were starting up this warehouse, but I didn't worry about how we assessed and selected our people. We hired great employees!"

How did the consultants do this? The answer has its roots in 310 pages of monotonous but critical professional and legal guidelines published by the *American Psychological Association (APA)*, the *Society for Industrial and Organizational Psychology (SIOP)*, and the *U.S. Equal Employment Opportunity Commission (EEOC)*.

Here are highlights from these guidelines...

Start with a *job analysis* to document what people do and KSAPCs (no surprise). Most Office of Federal Contracts and Compliance Programs (OFCCP) auditors will expect to see job analysis results, at a minimum... Have them ready!

The guidelines also stress the importance of two metrics related to assessment tool quality:

Reliability – A *reliable* car gets you where you want to go, every time. A reliable assessment tool produces (nearly) the same score—every time.

If a tool is unreliable, it cannot be valid.

Validity – While a reliable tool measures "something," validity determines whether the tool measures a skill that is critical to job performance.

Don't be fooled by marketing collateral. Just because a test produces a score doesn't mean the score has any value.

Say you're selecting firefighters based on KSAPCs and assessment tools below. The APA/SIOP guidelines describe three validation methods. Each method is presented in **bold text**, followed by examples:

- **Content Validation** – *Safety during forest fires (knowledge)*. Prepare a test with content that "matches" what a firefighter needs to know in this situation.
- **Content Validation** – *Using fire hydrants (skill)*. Candidates demonstrate what they need to do on the job using an actual fire hydrant.
    - Assumption – Expert assessors are trained to observe and evaluate candidates using relevant, standardized protocols.
- **Criterion-Related Validation** – *Problem solving (ability)*. Firefighter knowledge is *not* required. Collect data that shows firefighters with higher test scores are also better performers (and vice versa). A significant statistical relationship (correlation) between candidate scores and measures of job performance is required.
- **Construct Validation** – *Creativity (personal characteristic)*. Firefighter knowledge is *not* required. Test scores have a history of measuring and predicting on-the-job creativity for similar jobs in other parts of the region.

CYLINDER 2 – REWARDS

Another story.

Ed, an engineering manager, takes a seat in your cube. He's concerned about his direct report, Eli. Ed explains that Eli has one foot out the door.

"He's too critical to lose. Finding a replacement will be impossible. We need to give him more money."

Ed spent weeks "selling" a retention increase to company executives. The CEO agreed to a 3% ($3,000) annual increase. Ed proudly delivers the news to Eli.

Eli leaves six weeks later to broaden his skills and to support a company vision that aligns more closely with his personal values.

Ed finds a talented replacement in five weeks.

Nineteen exit interviews conducted *six months or more after employees left* tell the same story. "It wasn't the money."

Tom McMullen, Korn Ferry's Rewards Practice Leader, puts it perfectly:

> *"...financial rewards are often critical in getting workers in the door, but nonfinancial rewards tend to keep people in organizations."*

CONNECTING REWARDS TO STRATEGY

Rewards practices rely on a *rewards philosophy* to connect them to strategy. This is a "formal statement documenting the company's position about employee rewards. It explains the 'why' behind employee rewards and creates a framework for consistency (SHRM.org)."

Rewards philosophies often address issues like:

- Strategy and targeted customer market(s)
- Retention assumptions
- Benefits:
  - Financial
  - Health/Wellness
  - Perks
- Individual/Organizational performance
- Business critical issues:
  - Vital professions?
  - Key markets?
  - Geography?
- Equity and risk tolerance

Don't forget about non-monetary rewards like unexpected time off, flexible hours/locations, discounts, transit/parking, occasional praise, etc.

Consistently delivered rewards are like wallpaper to your workforce. Nobody even notices them until they change. Reducing them leads to widespread angst.

Change management helps soften the impact of reduced rewards. Kotter and ADKAR are useful change management models that can help mute an otherwise visceral workforce reaction to rewards changes.

CYLINDER 3 — STRUCTURE

Imagine working for a company that has established a competitive advantage in next-day delivery. Internal efficiencies rule the day.

Meetings start and end on time—and almost every meeting focuses on eliminating pesky exceptions. And profit soars.

Now, imagine a new SVP of Sales changing the organizational structure.

Confusion and frustration follow:

- Who approves price changes?
- Who's my new boss? (Yes—this really happens.)
- Why have customer complaints increased?
- Why is Competitor X "advertising" our problems?
- Why did our stock price drop?

While part of this mayhem is the result of poor change management, the rest comes from destroying familiar information and workflows.

"Hire great people and stay out of their way" is simply naïve. Even great people are susceptible to the crush of deeply embedded, inefficient or unknown workflows, wonky metrics, and market changes.

But structure is only one part of an integrated web of organizational features. Changing structure without changing workflows, internal customers, goals, jobs, etc. hobbles a company.

"Hire great people and stay out of their way" is simply naïve. Even great people are susceptible to the crush of deeply embedded, inefficient or unknown workflows, wonky metrics, and market changes.

This is the stuff of *organizational design* (OD).

Here are some important OD principles:

- Start with strategy and extract "must have" organizational competencies like:
    - unmatched program/project management or

- o   frictionless services supported by technology.
- Evaluate today's organizational competencies against the "must haves."
- Identify "must change, eliminate, or add" organizational features (IT, approval chains, etc.).
- Plan for each change, elimination, or addition.
  - o   *Remember change management!*
- Implement.
- *Stay engaged!* Monitoring and correcting are vital to success!

Results from OD efforts will never be perfect, but they're never permanent, either. OD is both an art and a science—and an invigorating professional challenge!

CYLINDER 4 — CULTURE

Watch what happens when you ask a group this question:

What is culture?

Uncomfortable giggles, averted gazes, and occasional looks of indignation follow. Sometimes the question comes back to you like a boomerang and you get to experience the same tension.

To be fair, Edgar Schein isn't convinced that culture should be defined:

> *"Culture" is a messy and divergent concept [...] it does not lend itself to clear definition and measurement.*

But, expected workforce behavior is a good starting point. It reflects the subconscious assumptions that employees accumulate over time.

Sara – "Why do we do this?"

Bill – "I don't know. There *must* be a reason, though."

Amazon doesn't publicize their strategy or culture, but they do publish a vision, guiding principles, and leadership principles (behaviors). Some excerpts:

- *Vision – The Most Customer-Centric Company on Earth*
- *Guiding Principles/Behaviors (Leadership Principles – LPs)*
    - *Guiding Principle 1 – Customer obsession rather than competitor focus*
        - *Behaviors – Customer obsession*
            - Start with the customer and work backwards.
            - Pay attention to competitors but obsess over customers.
    - *Guiding Principle 2 – Passion for invention*
        - *Behaviors – Invent and simplify*
            - Always find ways to simplify.
            - Look for new ideas from everywhere.

Amazon's recruiters ask interview questions that drill down on candidates' use of LPs in work situations. Their cylinders (performance, rewards, development) and day-to-day employee interactions are designed to:

- Extinguish behaviors that run counter to LPs, and
- Promote behavior that is consistent with LPs.

The "why" becomes embedded in widely-held, subconscious employee values (aka culture) and is only accessible by people from the outside (Schein).

Culture is susceptible to external forces, too. Location, industry ("law" versus "landscaping"), customers, and other external features can influence the way employees work.

Want to change culture? Focus on changing and aligning vision, values/guiding principles, and employee behavior. Embed all three in the six cylinders... and watch culture change over time.

CYLINDER 5 – PERFORMANCE

You're on a team charged with improving the company's performance management system. It doesn't take long before the whiteboard is *filled* with variables that impact performance management quality.

Scale points, timing, definitions, goals, and more.

However, the manager/employee dialogue is conspicuously missing, despite being the centerpiece of performance management. Everything else should make this dialogue better.

Strategy should fuel performance management through its two components:

1. *"The What" – Goals and responsibilities*
2. *"The How" – KSAPCs*

"The What" is shorthand for what an employee is expected to accomplish. It's represented by goals and responsibilities:

- *Goals* – The most valuable motivational tool in a manager's arsenal—"good" goals just work. What's a "good" goal? Specific, measurable, attainable, realistic, and time-bound (SMART). Noticeably missing—the connection between the goal and strategy (SMART*S!*).

  Is "lowest cost" part of your strategy? Consider a cost reduction goal. Entering new markets? Set goals that reflect attracting new customers.

This template helps create strategic goals:

Step 1 - <WHO?> is going to do <WHAT?> by <WHEN?> and <WHY?>.

Step 2 - <METRICS?>

- *Responsibilities* – "Blueprint Design and Management" is a responsibility. It might involve gathering requirements, choosing materials, using engineering standards, and quality checks. This content is usually found in job descriptions.

Goals and *responsibilities* should combine to cover most of an employee's job while avoiding a level of specificity that makes a meaningful dialogue difficult. Five to seven goals and/or responsibilities usually cover a job reasonably well.

"*The How*" is shorthand for critical KSAPCs like "Business Acumen" or "Collaboration." These can help to:

- reduce the likelihood of inappropriate behavior associated with meeting goals "at all costs," and
- provide a blueprint for development discussions.

CYLINDER 6 – DEVELOPMENT

Dale had a dilemma. She wanted to be a supervisor but had no experience managing a team.

She was an active member of the program committee for a local chamber of commerce. When it was time to find a new committee chair, she volunteered. She and the committee established an operating model, introduced networking events, and engaged chamber members in identifying program topics.

The year she spent leading the program committee developed her ability to manage and lead. The stories she told interviewers about running the committee were impressive. And she became a supervisor.

"MIND THE GAP" is a phrase that reminds London commuters to pay attention to the space between the train and the platform.

"MIND DEVELOPMENT GAPS" is far more complex. Development gaps are evident when:

- Performance standards are unmet.
- Employees transition to new roles.
- Strategy changes.
- Successors are considered.

There are several frameworks that can help expose performance expectations. Here's one that we use:

- *Business Strategy* – This has a direct impact on what employees are expected to do.
- *Structure and Job Tasks* – Information/workflow and job descriptions can help illuminate expected employee performance standards.
- *Internal and External Customers* – Customers know what they want. Just ask!
- *Culture* – A valuable source of internal norms regarding performance.
- *Performance Management* – A repository of performance expectations (and a starting point for finding development gaps).

WHEN PERFORMANCE FALLS SHORT OF EXPECTATIONS

Don't limit yourself to training!

Finding "the right" development activity to narrow performance gaps is an exercise in creativity. Here are just a few development solutions to get you started:

- Reading
- Video
- Coaching
- Mentoring
- Special projects
- Volunteer assignments
- Job shadowing

YOUR PLANE STARTS TO DESCEND...

The CEO next to you says, "That was an interesting chat! I took a lot of notes, but can you recap?"

Before you close the "I Create a Competitive Advantage" folder you opened, you say,

"Sure!

"I create a competitive advantage. Establishing a competitive advantage depends on the number of employees who a) understand their role in strategy execution, b) can contribute to strategy execution, and c) work diligently to do so. Plus, a good strategy.

"My role is to partner with CEOs and other managers to help them help employees with these three things. Both the business and its employees are better positioned to deliver a competitive advantage when employees have a specific blend of KSAPCs that connect to strategy.

"The 'People Engine' is how I think about creating a competitive advantage. Business strategy configures and fuels the engine's six cylinders:

1. *Selection* – 'Screens in' candidates with strategic KSAPCs.
2. *Rewards* – Reinforce strategic behavior.
3. *Structure* - Creates predictable information and workflows (along with OD).
4. *Culture* – Reinforces acceptable and extinguishes unacceptable behavior.
5. *Performance* – Establishes goals, responsibility, and KSAPC standards for workers.
6. *Development* – Enhances skills to narrow performance gaps.

"In the end, I help executives create an 'engine' that a) is as unique as their strategy, b) helps deliver what our customers need, and c) is very difficult for competitors to replicate.

"That's how I help my company win in the marketplace."

"I'll drink to that!" she replies. "Now, where's my torque wrench?"

You both have a good laugh!

She leaves the plane a more sophisticated HR consumer, and you leave content, knowing that another business leader is better equipped to deliver strategy through their employees!

Want more? Visit
https://www.talentalignment.net/thepeopleengine

Chapter 15

What Every Mentor Knows: "You Can't Google This Stuff!"

Dr. Pamela D. Grey

Thought Leader on How to Make Your Best Decisions
and Premier Mentor to Women in Business

poweryourdecisions.com

facebook.com/power.your.decisions

instagram.com/power.your.decisions

Dr. Pamela Grey's passion for life-building decisions positioned her to become a premier mentor for the Women's Leadership Alliance (WLA), an organization promoting women with careers in financial services. Her award-winning book, *Power Your Decisions Self-Study Workbook: A Personalized Roadmap to Success,* teaches all people how to make "WOW" decisions without any regret. Pamela achieved her doctorate by age thirty, later becoming a dean for long-range planning, research, and technology and an assistant scholar for higher education at the University of Florida. If one career wasn't enough, she went on to become a financial advisor to many families and businesses in a successful second career, a pathway that is still very challenging for women today. Within seven years, she formed her own company, Grey Investment Group, Inc., and navigated as its president for more than thirteen more years before pursuing a new, third chapter in her life—becoming a full-time writer, mentor to women in business, and spiritual coach to help people make their best decisions. Her workbook is also endorsed by all Centers for Spiritual Living. Sign up for Dr. Grey's free monthly newsletter, *Better Ideas for Better Decisions,* on her website: www.poweryourdecisions.com.

• • •

Everyone needs a mentor:

To make a transition into a new phase of life or career

To be told things that maybe they've suspected but haven't yet accepted

To partner with someone who clearly has been successful

To open their mind to new ideas

To confidentially share their weaknesses and strengths

To truly listen to someone with so much knowledge

To see themselves in a different light

To feel empowered to use skills that come to them naturally

To stop the feeling of isolation

Likely, you can recall tipping points in your life, some positive and some negative. These are times when you say to yourself, "What is the cost if I don't make a good decision?" Moments like these can land us in trouble and unfamiliar places if we don't assess our situation correctly. Who can we turn to at times like these? Who has experience with seismic shifts? It must be a person of great value, because *no* amount of money could buy their wisdom, or the poignant moments of guidance that make or break your success. And while you may not always appreciate their frankness, mentors can be your best catalysts for personal change. The following brief stories describe some of my experiences with such great mentors, individuals who turned everything around when I needed them most.

UNLOCKING DOORS TO MARVELOUS CHANGE

I found many doors of opportunity swing wide on the hinges of emotional competence. These doors can also shut quickly, without you knowing it, if you don't understand how your emotions are impacting your behaviors. A real eye-opener for me was discovering my own native intelligence—meaning a high IQ or excellent test scores—would not guarantee my success, but my emotional competence could. I was fortunate to meet Dr. Denise Federer, a behavioral psychologist and coach, early on. She asked me these insightful questions:

- Was I adaptable? Could I build trust easily?
- Did I exhibit empathy?
- Did I take initiative? Was I a team player?
- Had I influenced others positively?
- Did I foster a drive for achievement?

Upon honest reflection, I could see important changes I needed to make. However, I also discovered I was resistant to some of those changes. She explained what held me back:

- Unclear motivation; not knowing what drives me
- Conflicting or competing values when dealing with difficult people
- Self-limiting thoughts or beliefs about myself
- Fear of the unknown in new situations
- Avoiding pain and discomfort when under pressure

None of these should surprise you. They stop all of us at one time or another. But my mentors helped me see how my current competencies and strengths had brought me this far. There was hope! They also took the time to point out that some of my goals were no longer a good fit, and they suggested I clean up my personal workspace and get my office better organized, too.

"Don't let a lack of order or good systems put your progress in jeopardy, Pamela," they said to me.

So, before you walk out on a limb or do something new, don't do what I did: pray every day God would build a tree underneath me! Instead, call your mentor for guidance! Once you go down a path to personal change, new doors of opportunity are bound to open with greater regularity. You won't have to push *so hard* if you just pick up the keys to marvelous change and unlock your unique gifts and talents. I found his simple affirmation helped me stay open-minded and more focused:

I AM WILLING to be flexible, organized, and aware of what changes *I need* to make. I prepare myself daily for stimulating new ideas I can act on with enthusiasm and clarity. I am open to marvelous changes that reward my time, gifts, and talents exceptionally well over time.

KNOW THE DIFFERENCE BETWEEN YOUR DREAMS AND A VISION

While in Orlando, Florida, I saw "The American Adventure," a special exhibit on how America was formed. What struck me during the performance was a dialogue between poet and author Mark Twain and Dr. Benjamin Franklin, one of the founding fathers of our country and a prolific inventor. During this drama about America's struggles, victories, and challenges in forming its alliances and the composition of the Constitution, Twain remarks to Franklin, "You had quite a dream for the country." Franklin quickly replied, "It was no dream. *We had a vision!*"

I was struck by the stark contrast between the words *dream* and *vision*. In the insightful book, *Creative Mind and Success*, Dr. Ernest Holmes, a true visionary in his own right, states, "Our word has the exact amount of power that we put into it." So, I concluded that

Franklin's word, "*vision*," must have held a lot of weight. He wanted all new Americans to secure the opportunities of a promised land.

Whether you are starting out on a new adventure or staying the course where you are, ask for a mentor's guidance. They will help you navigate unfamiliar terrain and new circumstances. They will point out when your ambitions, hopes, and wishes are more like dreams, when what you really need is a clear vision. You can imagine a vision, but what you truly *feel* are your dreams. ***Over time, both are needed, but a daydream is no substitute for taking real action!***

Now would be a great time to ask yourself if you have a clear vision. Are you being forward-thinking? Once you get past the daydreaming, a clear vision is *your* call to action! Our founders knew this! They also understood that a vision takes time to be realized. Sometimes they don't turn out like we first imagine them. That is okay, if progress is being made.

Mentors can and will help you put all the details on your roadmap to success. They know your vision is filled with great passion. They will cheer you on and point out all your milestones, even when you don't see them. A good mentor is someone who is very wise, thoughtful, and visionary—and someone you most admire. At critical times in your life, especially when these seismic shifts require good decision-making, it will be their words you hold onto to help you keep both eyes on *the prize!*

EVERYTHING HAS HAPPENED FOR YOU

"My past did not happen to me, but *for me*. Everything in life has happened *for me*."

These words really resonated with me. In his book *Personality Isn't Permanent*, Dr. Benjamin Hardy led me to a profound realization: Don't repeat your past; repeat only what works for you. At the time, I was changing careers, and a long-time mentor offered me a book he said would change my life: *The Power of Decision* by Dr. Raymond

Charles Barker. I was skeptical at first, until I read it. Dr. Barker said that to make even better decisions, you must pay a price. The price of giving up your hurts, errors, negative assertions, and self-righteousness to become a better version of yourself. That was a *big ask* for me at the time!

So, was I to believe everything had happened *for me*? Would I be willing to pay an even higher price to reach a new level of success? After reading both books, I was convinced the answer to both was *yes*. But Dr. Barker also left me one warning I cannot forget. He said people weep far too long over the past and what could have been, had they been wiser. He said this is not only a useless contemplation, but also a negative one.

I was totally on board: regretting the past would put everything in jeopardy. What was more helpful was to look at where my decisions had already led me. Oh, how many thoughtful conversations with mentors made the difference between my success and failure. If things were falling apart, they helped me make sense of it all; they knew what to do. The moral of my story is that there is no value in just what happened to you, because what happened *for you* is much more significant.

Well, how did my new career choice turn out? After jumping into corporate life, my confidence was quickly shaken, and I started to regret my decision to leave my career of seventeen years behind. However, I got up the courage to call my former college president before I jumped ship. In a reassuring tone, he said to me, "Pamela, God did not bring you this far to drop you!"

Oh, how my world stopped spinning around! He explained that my second career would be a resounding success, especially since my first career in higher education had been so exceptional. *Everything was happening for me, not to me!* In the twenty-two years that followed, I became president and CEO of my own financial company and enjoyed a lucrative career! At the end of the day, everything *had* truly happened *for me*.

Before you get caught up in a cycle of fear or regret because you have taken on a new challenge, remind yourself the past has happened *for you*. Experience is a strength. All your previous decisions are simply stepping stones. Keep those words and wise truths ever present in your mind, and remember, God did not bring you this far to drop you! Relax and stop to smell the roses. And don't forget to continue to remind yourself, *Just look how far I've come!*

TAKE YOUR CUE FROM THE MULTIVERSE

If you have ever done yoga, you realize stretching is good for your body. Flexibility is also necessary for your mental health and outlook as well. Younger friends, travel, and taking courses are very beneficial, but are often not enough to prepare you for greater challenges. In their book *365 Days of Richer Living*, Drs. Ernest Holmes and Raymond Charles Barker explain that the universe—now called a multiverse—is made up of ever-expanding systems. These systems are pliant and flexible, growing wider and wider to realize *their* fullest potential. So, while nature is expanding the whole multiverse, why not take your cue to morph into something even greater yourself? Could the cosmos be telling you something?

One spiritual mentor explained to me that God is never trapped in its own creation. *What a brilliant concept!* I said to myself. So, that means I can never be trapped in my own circumstances. I can never be restricted or have limits placed on my choices. But if some part of me shuts down or, worse yet, is being neglected, I turn to the guidance of a mentor. They never allow me to suffer silently without making some positive suggestions.

I have chosen to personalize this truth about God and call *It* my own Creative Intelligence. This Intelligence gives me new ideas and imaginative ways to solve all my problems. But ideas alone won't bring me better solutions if I am not willing to act on them. That is the key—*to be responsive!* I've always said I was born with average intelligence, but was given above-average curiosity! Being adventurous and curious has been a secret to my success in so many new instances.

Another point I want to make is that I believe a Creative Intelligence runs the whole cosmos. This means I take my cue from a multiverse that keeps expanding. It also means I cannot stay static or remain too long in my comfort zone. Funny how my little corner of the multiverse won't expand if *I* don't. Frequently, it all boils down to a closed mind to new opportunities. This is when I throw out all the laws of nature and believe I know better. My world stops spinning in a hot minute if I don't remind myself to keep moving. If you want to see new opportunities appearing on your horizon, use your curiosity and take in new information. Finally, be sure to observe all the laws of nature around you!

LEAVE ALL YOUR PAPER TIGERS BEHIND

If a loss or personal setback in your private life or career has occurred, you likely feel your happiness and joy have been negatively impacted. You are not alone. The worst part is when your paper tigers come out to taunt you. At first glance, paper tigers seem threatening, even terrifying. In the end, though, they lack any real power to take away your peace of mind. When a paper tiger shows up in your life or career, baring its sharp teeth and claws, ask your mentor for an exit strategy so that you are not eaten alive.

Mentors often remind us we do have choices. We don't need to panic. For example, if a great job opportunity did not materialize or a decision caused you pain, don't despair. This is a great opportunity to ask for help. Years ago, when I was in the throes of a major setback, I shared all my pain with a mentor. After a good cry, she said to me in a matter-of-fact voice, "Pamela, your good is *not* being withheld from you."

I was frozen and unable to think. How could she be so certain? She had all the nitty-gritty about how I lost my job! I simply was not ready to embrace her words of wisdom. When she said my good was not being withheld, I was emotionally too absorbed in my loss to truly listen to someone with so much knowledge. I sulked for a few more weeks before my whining spree came to a sudden halt. I realized my goal was not to *stop* there. This was *not* the end of the line! Somehow, all my paper tigers had come out to roam and, bite after bite, I thought my good was being taken away. It had only *appeared* that way.

Thankfully, mentors can show you how to turn negative encounters around. Amid our quandaries and confused thinking, they help us see so clearly what we cannot see for ourselves. So, if a paper tiger jumps out at you, do not let it back you into a corner. Even if that does occur, it's not Ghostbusters you should call! It's your mentor.

The next time a mentor softly whispers in your ear, "Your good is not being withheld from you," listen to them. Don't moan or groan. *Stop*, before you open that next door that might allow *your* paper tigers to roam!

WHAT DOES SUCCESS MEAN TO YOU?

In a favorite book of mine by Dr. Ernest Holmes, *A New Design for Living*, he says we are all successful at reaching our goals. He points out some people are terrific at always being a failure in business. Others succeed in experiencing poor health all the time. And some people are very good at being friendless. The immediate problem is not one of success; rather, what kind of success is worth having? Dr. Holmes also reminds us to periodically reassess our results. Look very closely at what kind of success you are experiencing. Do your results represent your best efforts? Are you getting positive feedback? Or is a deeper issue causing you to be stressed? Whatever your situation, it is always good to look at your results when they show up.

As a business owner in my second career, I paid a lot of attention to my client relationships, my employees' development, and how to run a profitable financial services company. Thankfully, I came across one simple formula for continuous improvement. I would ask myself at the end of each day, "What could I do better? What did I have control over?" Once I answered these questions, I would repeat what worked and discard everything else.

With the aid of my mentors, I never lost sight of the kind of success that's worth having. Perhaps a simple formula of asking yourself if you are happy with your results could work for you. As you consciously shift away from conditions or circumstances that no longer serve you, new opportunities will arise to help you achieve even greater success. The goal is to experience an underlying sense of fulfillment that takes you far beyond most ordinary goals. Keep that clearly in mind.

If it were not for my mentors cheering me on, many milestones would not have been achieved. I was fortunate that I listened to their experiences and embraced their truths. Yet, in the end, I was the one to move my daydreams closer to a vision. I was the one who remained flexible and had the courage to walk through new doors. I picked up the keys to marvelous change that were handed to me at difficult times. And I chose to unlock my gifts and talents that would lead to better choices and even better decisions, just in the nick of time.

So, when you take on a new challenge, find yourself a trusted mentor before you experience seismic shifts or navigate the harrowing demands of whitewater events. That said, be discerning with your choice, and take your time choosing a mentor who personalizes their guidance and offers great wisdom only from *lived experiences*. Above all else, pay close attention to the one mentor who already knows... *you can't Google this stuff!*

Conclusion

We hope you have enjoyed this *When Work Works* and the fresh perspectives of each of the authors. We've journeyed through diverse perspectives on what makes work truly work. There's no single formula for success, but the variety of insights we've explored sheds light on the many paths to creating thriving workplaces.

But this anthology isn't just a collection of ideas—it's a roadmap for action, urging us to champion our people, prioritize well-being, and embrace flexibility to shape a better world of work.

So let's take these insights to heart and drive change. Let's celebrate our differences, nurture well-being, and adapt to new ways of working. Together, we can build workplaces where everyone can flourish.

Call for Submissions

Would you like to be included in our next anthology? Do you have a message that needs to be shared with the world? Would you like to see your work published and enjoy the benefits that come from authorship?

Whether you are in the development stage or already have a complete manuscript, simply reach out to Cathy Fyock at Cathy@CathyFyock.com. She would be happy to speak with you about your manuscript and your mission.

SHRM Foundation

Proceeds from the sale of this book will be provided to the SHRM Foundation.

The SHRM Foundation mobilizes HR and employers to tackle the complex societal issues that affect the workplace. As the nonprofit arm of SHRM, the world's largest HR association, SHRM Foundation empowers and equips HR to build a more inclusive talent pipeline, address the crisis of mental health and wellness, and prepare for the next big challenge. With a unique capacity to engage employers in solutions, SHRM Foundation partners with companies, foundations, nonprofits and government to drive research-informed programs, leadership coalitions and peer support for SHRM's 340,000 members and beyond. Together, we are building a world of work that works for all, where all talent and workplaces prosper and thrive.

For more information, visit https://www.shrm.org/foundation.

About the Editors

ABOUT CATHY FYOCK

Cathy Fyock is The Business Book Strategist and works with professionals and thought leaders who want to write a book as a business and career growth strategy. She began her career as an HR professional.

She is the author of twelve books. Her early books focused on her work in employment issues for older workers and strategies for recruiting and retaining employees. Her last books focus on her work as a book coach, including:

- *On Your Mark: From First Word to First Draft in Six Weeks*
- *Blog2Book: Repurposing Content to Discover the Book You've Already Written*
- *The Speaker Author: Sell More Books and Book More Speeches*
- *Authority: Strategic Concepts from 15 International Thought Leaders*
- *My New Book: The Upcoming Message that Will Change the World*
- *Writer Crisis Hotline: The Write Solutions for Authors*

When Work Works is her tenth HR and leadership anthology; Cathy loves working with aspiring authors to create their first or next book.

ABOUT THE EDITORS

Since starting her book coaching business in 2014, she's helped more than 200 professionals become published authors—the work she is called to do.

She believes that authors can and do change the world, one word at a time.

If you know of someone who is interested in exploring authorship, reach out to Cathy at Cathy@CathyFyock.com.

ABOUT THE EDITORS

ABOUT EVERETT O'KEEFE

Everett O'Keefe is a Wall Street Journal, USA Today, and International #1 Bestselling Author. *The Power of the Published* is his most recent solo work. He has also helped create and launch more than 150 bestselling books for his clients. Everett speaks across the nation on the power of publishing. He is the founder of Ignite Press, a hybrid publishing company that specializes in helping entrepreneurs, as well as business and medical professionals, ignite their businesses by becoming bestselling authors.

Everett is the winner of multiple awards, including the Publish and Profit Award for Excellence in Publishing, the Make Market & Launch It Award for Product Creation, and the Top Gun Consulting Award, among others. He is the co-founder of the Business Accelerator Group, a high-level mastermind group composed of international marketers and publishers. He also founded the Mastermind Retreat and hosts international mastermind events.

In 2019, Everett founded The Book Publishers Network, a group of publishers, publishing consultants, book coaches and other book professionals. In 2020, he founded The Publishers Mastermind in order to help support publishing professionals from around the world.

Everett is sought out as a speaker, coach, and consultant by authors and marketing experts worldwide. With a passion for entrepreneurialism, Everett helps his clients become recognized experts in their fields through speaking and authorship while allowing his clients to focus on their own areas of giftedness.

You can reach Everett through his company's website at https://IgnitePress.us.

Everett can also be found on social media at these sites:

https://www.facebook.com/ignitepress/
https://www.linkedin.com/in/everettokeefe/
https://www.instagram.com/ignitepress.us/

Made in the USA
Middletown, DE
03 August 2024